THE WORLD OF MUSIC
MOZART
AND HIS WORLD

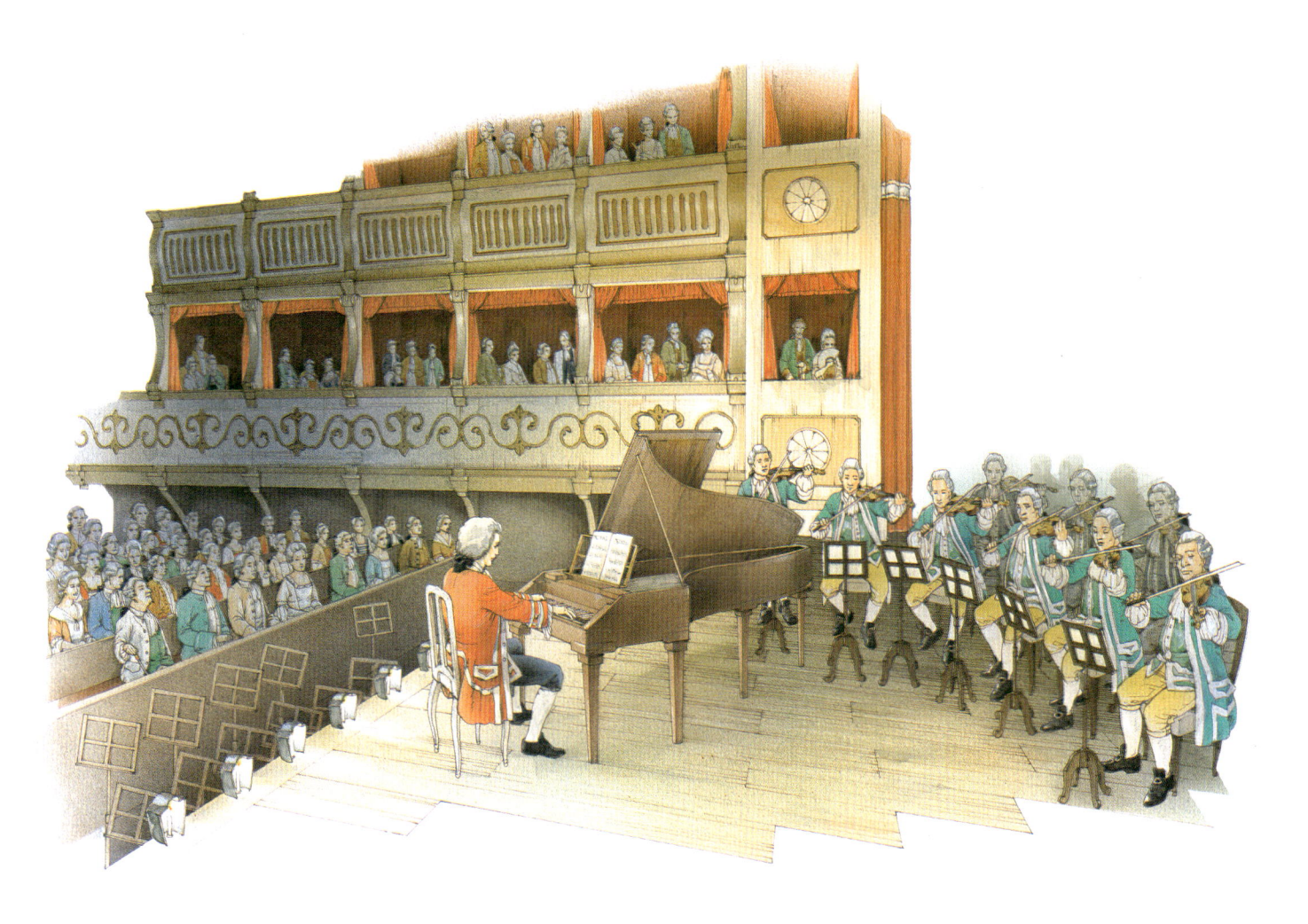

Text by
Francesco Salvi

Illustrations by
L.R. Galante, Manuela Cappon
Studio Boni-Pieri-Critone

W
FRANKLIN WATTS
NEW YORK · LONDON · SYDNEY

DoGi

This edition
first published in
Great Britain in 1998

Franklin Watts
96 Leonard Street
London EC2A 4RH

Franklin Watts Australia
14 Mars Road
Lane Cove
NSW 2066

ISBN 0 7496 3291 7

A CIP catalogue record
for this book is available
from the British Library

English translation
© Copyright 1998 by
Barrons Educational
Series Inc

Original edition
© Copyright 1997 by
DoGi s.r.l., Florence, Italy

Printed in Italy

All rights reserved.

Originally published as
Mozart e il suo tempo

Written by
Francesco Salvi

Illustrations by
L. R. Galante,
Manuela Cappon,
Studio Boni-Pieri-Critone

Illustration Design:
Francesco Lo Bello

Art direction
and page make-up:
Sebastiano Ranchetti

Picture research:
Katherine Carson Forden

Editorial staff:
Andrea Bachini,
Renzo Rossi

English translation by
Anna Maria Salmeri-
Pherson

HOW TO READ THIS BOOK

Every facing page is a chapter on Mozart's musical art and life, the great events of the musical culture of his times, or a detailed analysis of the instruments and/or the theory of the musical art. The text above on the left (1) and the large illustration in the middle, deal with the main subject. The text in italics (2) recounts in chronological order the life of Mozart. The other elements on the page—photos, reproductions of prints of the time, and portraits—complement the information.

ACKNOWLEDGMENTS

ABBREVIATIONS
t: (top)/ b: (below) / c: (center) / r: (right) / l: (left)
AKG: ARCHIV FÜR KUNST UND GESCHICHTE, BERLIN.
ILLUSTRATIONS: The illustrations displayed in this volume are new and original. They have been realized upon a project by DoGi s.r.l., that owns its copyright.
LIST OF THE REPRODUCTIONS:
DoGi s.r.l. has done its best to discover possible rights of third parties. We apologize for any omissions or mistakes that might have occurred, and we will be pleased to introduce the appropriate corrections in the later editions of this book.
We would like to thank the Accademia Bartolomeo Cristofori in Florence for its collaboration.
(The works reproduced in their integrity are followed by the consonant a (all); those partially reproduced are followed by the consonant d (detail);

6d Pietro Antonio Lorenzoni (attributed), *Leopold Mozart*, c.1765, unsigned oil portrait, (INTERNATIONALE STIFTUNG MOZARTEUM, SALZBURG) d; **8d** Martin van Meytens, *Maria Theresa, German Empress, Queen of Hungary and Bohemia*, 1717, painting (SCHLOSS SCHÖNBRUNN, VIENNA; AKG/ERICH LESSING, BERLIN) a; **9tr** Christian Homeman, *Portrait of Ludwig van Beethoven as a youth*, painting, 1803 (ARCHIVIO DoGi, FLORENCE) a; **11tr** Kurt Remshard after drawings by Anton Danreiter, *The Cathedral of Salzburg*, engraving (ARCHIVIO DoGi, FLORENCE) a; **11cr** Johann Michael Grieter, *Hieronymus von Colloredo* (AKG, BERLIN) d; **12tl** Angelo Crescimbeni, *Padre Martini*, second half of the eighteenth century, oil painting (CIVICO MUSEO BIBLIOGRAFICO MUSICALE, BOLOGNA) d; **13tl** C. Silvestri, *Arcangelo Corelli*, engraving (ST. MARK'S NATIONAL LIBRARY, VIENNA) a(ll); **13cr** *The Diploma of Mozart in Bologna*, 1770 (INTERNATIONALE STIFTUNG MOZARTEUM, SALZBURG) a; **13tr** Anonymous, *Mozart with the Golden Spur*, painting (CIVICO MUSEO BIBLIOGRAFICO MUSICALE, BOLOGNA) d; **14tl** *Italian Spinet*, end of the eighteenth century (ACCADEMIA BARTOLOMEO CRISTOFORI, FLORENCE) a; **14cl** *Virginal*, end of the nineteenth century (ACCADEMIA BARTOLOMEO CRISTOFORI, FLORENCE) a; **14cr** Hans Ruckers, *Two Manuals Flemish Harpsichord*, c.1625 (ACCADEMIA BARTOLOMEO CRISTOFORI, FLORENCE) a; **14c** *Mozart's Harpsichord* (INTERNATIONALE STIFTUNG MOZARTEUM, SALZBURG) a; **14br** *Two-Manual Harpsichord by Horst Rase*, (ACCADEMIA BARTOLOMEO CRISTOFORI, FLORENCE) a; **15tc** G. Schüler, *Clavichord Concerto*, 1794 (AKG, BERLIN) a; **15tr** *Modern Piano by Steinway* (STEINWAY & SONS, HAMBURG) a; **15bl** *Gravicembalo col piano e forte by Bartolomeo Cristofori* [Harpsichord with soft and loud by Bartolomeo Cristofori], 1720, (THE METROPOLITAN MUSEUM OF ART, NEW YORK) a(ll); **15br** *Harpsichord by Johann Andreas Stein*, 1775, (ACCADEMIA BARTOLOMEO CRISTOFORI, FLORENCE) a; **16tl** Josef Kreutzinger, Carlo Artaria, Publisher, 1780, painting, 27.5" × 31.4", (MUSEEN DER STADT, VIENNA, AKG/ERICH LESSING, BERLIN) a; **16c** Carl Schütz, *The Premises of Artaria & Co.*, 1786, engraving (BRITISH LIBRARY, LONDON) d; **17tr** *Portrait of Maria Anna Thekla Mozart*, engraving (INTERNATIONALE STIFTUNG MOZARTEUM, SALZBURG) d; **18d** Anonymous (MUSEEN DER STADT) d; **20d** Anonymous, *Portrait of Giovanni Battista Pergolesi*, painting (PINACOTECA CIVICA, JESI) d; **21tc** Domenico Oliviero, *Inside the Teatro Regio of Turin*, oil painting, 50.3" × 44.8", (MUSEO CIVICO D'ARTE ANTICA AND PALAZZO MADAMA, TURIN) d; **22tl** Joseph Siffred Duplessis, *Christoph Willibald Gluck at the Spinet*, 1775, oil painting (KUNSTHISTORISCHES MUSEUM, VIENNA; AKG/ERICH LESSING, BERLIN) d; **24d** Anonymous, *Haydn in Prince Paul Anton Esterházy's house uniform*, (MUSEEN DER STADT, VIENNA); **25b** Anonymous, *Nicolaus Esterházy "the Magnificent"*, c.1770-87, in oils, 78.7" × 56.8", (NATIONAL HUNGARIAN GALLERY, BUDAPEST); **25tc** Anonymous, *Johann Peter Salomon* (Igda, MILAN) d; **28d** Title Page of the original production of *Idomeneo*, 1781 (AKG, BERLIN); **29t** *Königliche Hoftheater*, lithography, 1840 (BILDARCHIV PREUSSISCHER KULTURBESITZ, BERLIN); **30bl** *Burgtheater*, Vienna (AKG/KARL HASENAUER, BERLIN); **31** Bernardo Bellotto, *View of Vienna from the Belvedere*, 1700–25, in oils, 53.1" × 83.8", (KUNSTHISTORISCHES MUSEUM, VIENNA) d; **33d** Bernardo Bellotto, *Schottenkirche, South-Eastern View of Vienna*, 1758–61, oil painting, 45.6" × 59.8", (KUNSTHISTORISCHES MUSEUM, VIENNA; AKG/ERICH LESSING, BERLIN) d; **33tr** Title Page of *Die Entführung aus dem Serail* (AKG, BERLIN) a; **33br** Anonymous, *Gottlieb Stephanie*, engraving (MUSEEN DER STADT, VIENNA) d; **34t** Johann Ziegler after Lorenz Janscha, *The Prater*, engraving, c.1794 (ARCHIVIO DoGi, FLORENCE) d; **35tr** Denis Diderot and Jean-Baptiste Le Rond D'Alembert, *Encyclopédie, vol. 5, Lutes' display*, table VII, a; **37tr** *Violin by Giuseppe Guarneri* (Igda, MILAN) d; **37br** *Violin by Antonio Stradivari*, 1715 (CREMONA, TOWN HALL) a; **39d** J.B. von Lampi, *Aloysia Weber stage-dressed as Zémire*, 1784, oil painting (INTERNATIONALE STIFTUNG MOZARTEUM, SALZBURG) d; **42tl** Anonymous, *Lorenzo Da Ponte*, engraving (FOTOTECA STORICA NATIONALE) d; **42c** Martin van Meyten, *Celebration of the Marriage between Joseph II with Isabel of Parma on October 10, 1760* (SCHLOSS SCHÖNBRUNN, VIENNA, AKG, BERLIN) a; **44tl** P.S. De Creuze, *Portrait of Pierre-Augustin Caron de Beaumarchais* (MUSÉE DE VERSAILLES; Igda, MILAN) d; **44bl** Georg Mahall, *The Marriage of Figaro, the Count's Kissing the Hand of the Countess*, 1794, Prague, engraving (ÖSTERREICHISCHES THEATERMUSEUM, VIENNA; FOTOVOUK) d; **45tr** *Stage dresses for a Nineteenth-century performance of the Marriage of Figaro* (MUSEEN DER STADT, VIENNA) a; **46t** *Ticket for a Concert by Mozart* (INTERNATIONALE STIFTUNG MOZARTEUM, SALZBURG) a; **47bl** Edward Scriven, *Muzio Clementi*, engraving (Igda, MILAN) d; **47br** Anonymous, *Anton Stadler's silhouette* (ARCHIV DER GESELLSCHAFT DER MUSIKFREUNDE, VIENNA) a; **49tr** V. Morstadt (attributed) *The Nostiz Theater*, c.1830-40, colored engraving, 4.92" × 7.08", (SALBURGER MUSEUM CAROLINUM AUGUSTEUM, SALZBURG) a; **50tl** Title Page of the first edition of the libretto of *Don Giovanni* (GESELLSCHAFT DER MUSIKFREUNDE, VIENNA) a; **51tr** Anonymous, *Don Giovanni and Leporello*, c.1825, colored engraving (ÖSTERREICHISCHES THEATER MUSEUM, VIENNA; FOTOVOUK) a; **51br** Anonymous, *Don Giovanni and Zerlina*, c.1825, colored engraving (ÖSTERREICHISCHES THEATER MUSEUM, VIENNA; FOTOVOUK) a; **52tbl** Anonymous, *Masonic Symbols, details of different aprons, eighteenth century*, silk (AKG, BERLIN) d; **53tr** Anonymous, *The Viennese Lodge* (MUSEEN DER STADT, VIENNA), d; **54tl** Philipp Richter, *Emanuel Schikaneder*, engraving (ARCHIVIO DoGi, FLORENCE) d; **55tr** Title Page of *The Magic Flute* (GESELLSCHAFT DER MUSIKFREUNDE, VIENNA) a; **56tl** Anonymous, *Antonio Salieri*, oil portrait (GESELLSCHAFT DER MUSIKFREUNDE, VIENNA) d; **56tr** J. Wohlmuth, *The Rauhensteingasse in Vienna with the house in which Mozart died*, c.1820, watercolor (INTERNATIONALE STIFTUNG MOZARTEUM, SALZBURG) a; **57tl** Johann Ziegler, *View of St. Mark's*, colored engraving (GRAPHISCHE SAMMLUNG ALBERTINA, VIENNA) a; **57tr** Anonymous, *Leopold II*, engraving (Idga, MILAN) d; **57b** Anonymous, *Joseph II*, engraving (Idga, MILAN) d; **58tl** *Monument to Mozart* (INTERNATIONALE STIFTUNG MOZARTEUM, SALZBURG) a; **59tr** Joseph Lange, *Constanze Mozart*, portrait in oils, 1782 (INTERNATIONALE STIFTUNG MOZARTEUM, SALZBURG) d; **60cl** *Mozart's chocolate candies* (ARCHIVIO DoGi/CARLO CANTINI, FLORENCE) a; **60tr** Anonymous, *Ludwig van Beethoven*, oil painting (Igda, MILAN) a; **60cr** *Herbert von Karajan* (RCS-Igda, MILAN) d; **60br** Scene from the movie *Amadeus* directed by Milos Forman, 1984 (SOUL KAENTZ COMPANY, LONDON, COURTESY OF KOBAL COLLECTION) a; **61tl** Caroline Bardua, *Carl Maria von Weber*, oil painting (AKG/BERLIN) d; **61tc** James Warren Childe, *Jacob Felix Mendelssohn Bartholdy*, 1829, watercolor (MENDELSSOHN ARCHIV) d; **61tr** *Gustav Mahler*, c.1905, painting (ARCHIVO DoGi, FLORENCE) a; **61cl** *Igor Stravinsky*, (FOTO ERICH AUERBACH) d; **61c** *Bruno Walter* (ÖSTERREICHISCHE NATIONAL BIBLIOTHEK, VIENNA) a; **61cr** *Elisabeth Schwarzkopf* (BOB WILLOUGHBY/REDFERNS, LONDON) d; **61bl** *Glenn Gould* (ARCHIVO DoGi, FLORENCE) d; **61bc** *View of Glyndebourne* (GLYNDEBOURNE, CITY OF GLYNDEBOURNE, PRESS OFFICE; GRAVETT PICTURE INDEX) a; **61br** *The Beatles* (HARD DAYS NIGHT PREMIERE, LONDON; REDFERNS, PHOTO: S&G) a

COVER (from left to right): 1. Pietro Antonio Lorenzoni (attributed) *Mozart at six years old*, 1763, oil painting (SALZBURG, INTERNATIONALE STIFTUNG MOZARTEUM) d; 2. Julius Nisle, *Don Giovanni, finale of Act I*, watercolor lithography, 1841 (ARCHIVIO DoGi, FLORENCE) d; 3. Johann Nepomuk Della Croce, *The Mozarts*, 1781, oil painting (INTERNATIONALE STIFTUNG MOZARTEUM, SALZBURG) d; 4. Franz Schmutzer, *Vienna*, oil painting (MUSEEN DER STADT, VIENNA) d

QUADRANT OF COVER
Anonymous, *Portrait of W. A. Mozart* (GESELLSCHAFT DER MUSIKFREUNDE, VIENNA) d.

CONTENTS

- 4 - The Protagonists
- 6 - The Apprenticeship
- 8 - The Child Prodigy
- 10 - Salzburg
- 12 - The Italian Musical Environment
- 14 - From Harpsichord to Piano
- 16 - Musicians and Music Publishers
- 18 - The Journey
- 20 - The Opera World
- 22 - Paris
- 24 - Haydn
- 26 - The Modern Orchestra
- 28 - How a Theater Works
- 30 - Vienna
- 32 - "Turkomania"
- 34 - The Entertainment
- 36 - Chamber Music
- 38 - Teaching
- 40 - The Sonata Form
- 42 - The Librettists
- 44 - The Marriage of Figaro
- 46 - The Concerto
- 48 - Prague
- 50 - Don Giovanni
- 52 - Freemasonry
- 54 - The Magic Flute
- 56 - A Pauper's Grave
- 58 - The Requiem
- 60 - The Myth
- 62 - Index of Mozart's Works
- 64 - General Index

THE PROTAGONISTS

During the second half of the eighteenth century, the role of musicians changed. For the first time in history, they were considered freelance professionals who claimed their rights for creative autonomy and freedom from exclusive bondage to the courts and the church. The music, the instruments, and the way of playing them all changed. In the Vienna of Joseph II, the style called "classical" became popular, thanks to a few composers. Wolfgang Amadeus Mozart, one of the greatest musical geniuses of all times, was its fervent protagonist.

♦ **HIS SISTER-IN-LAW** Aloysia Weber (1761–1839), Constanze's older sister, an excellent singer.

♦ **THE COUSIN** Maria Anna Thekla Mozart (1758–1841), young Wolfgang's companion.

♦ **THE POWERFUL** Hieronymus von Colloredo (1732–1812), the Archbishop of Salzburg.

♦ **THE WIFE** Constanze Weber (1762–1842) married Mozart in 1782.

♦ **NANNERL** Maria Anna (1751–1829), Wolfgang's older sister, affectionately called Nannerl.

♦ **THE PARENTS** Leopold Mozart (1719–1787), a skilled musician, Vice Court Conductor (*Vice-Kapellmeister*) for the Archbishop of Salzburg. He married Anna Maria Pertl (1720–1778).

♦ **MOZART** Wolfgang Amadeus Mozart, born in Salzburg in 1756. He died in Vienna in 1791 at the age of 35.

♦ **JOSEPHA DUŠEK** Bohemian singer who opened her home in Prague to Mozart in 1787. The musician fell in love with her.

♦ **THE REGENTS** Maria Theresa, Empress of Austria (1717–1780). After her death, her son, Joseph II (1741–1790).

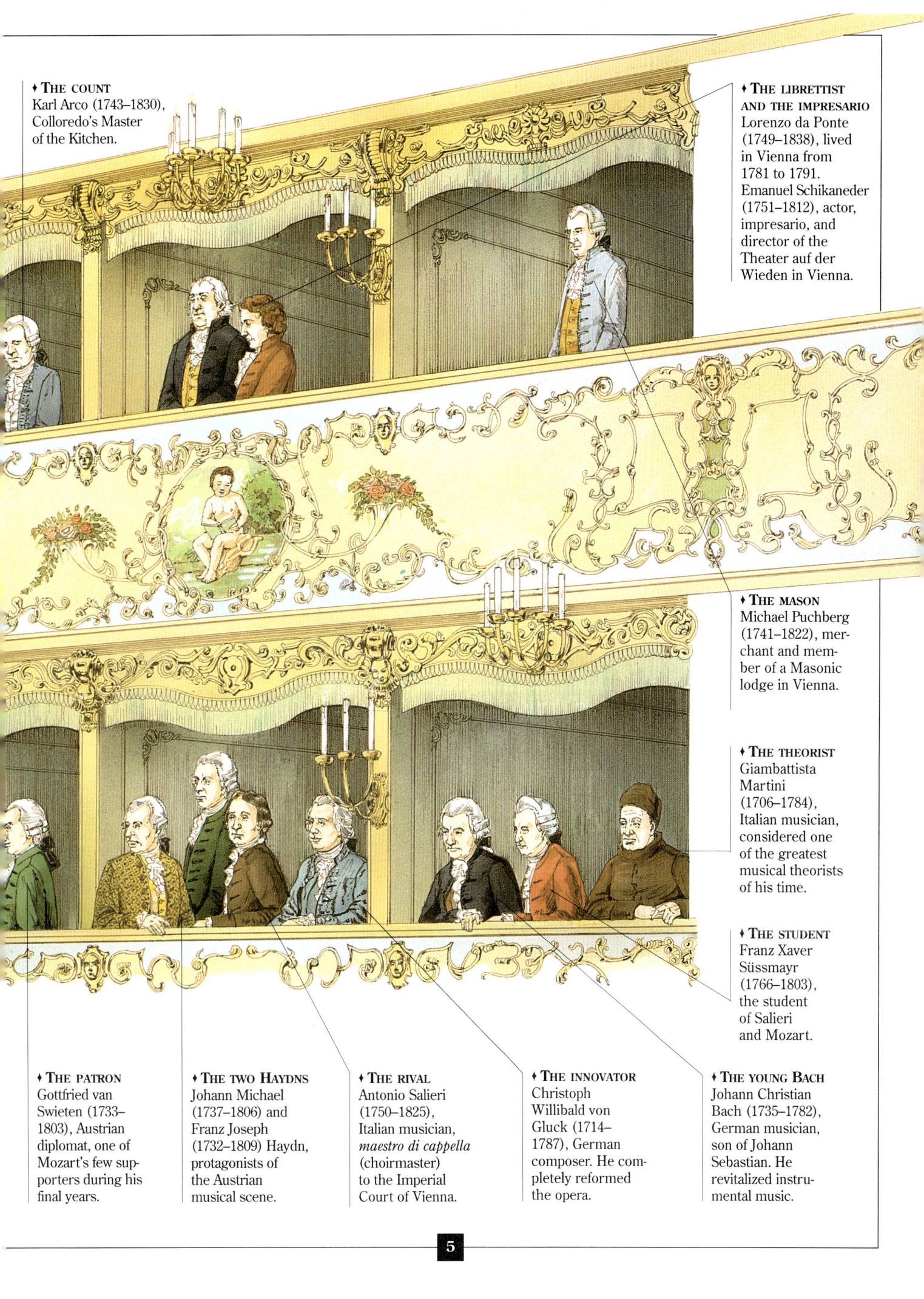

♦ **THE COUNT**
Karl Arco (1743–1830), Colloredo's Master of the Kitchen.

♦ **THE LIBRETTIST AND THE IMPRESARIO**
Lorenzo da Ponte (1749–1838), lived in Vienna from 1781 to 1791. Emanuel Schikaneder (1751–1812), actor, impresario, and director of the Theater auf der Wieden in Vienna.

♦ **THE MASON**
Michael Puchberg (1741–1822), merchant and member of a Masonic lodge in Vienna.

♦ **THE THEORIST**
Giambattista Martini (1706–1784), Italian musician, considered one of the greatest musical theorists of his time.

♦ **THE STUDENT**
Franz Xaver Süssmayr (1766–1803), the student of Salieri and Mozart.

♦ **THE PATRON**
Gottfried van Swieten (1733–1803), Austrian diplomat, one of Mozart's few supporters during his final years.

♦ **THE TWO HAYDNS**
Johann Michael (1737–1806) and Franz Joseph (1732–1809) Haydn, protagonists of the Austrian musical scene.

♦ **THE RIVAL**
Antonio Salieri (1750–1825), Italian musician, *maestro di cappella* (choirmaster) to the Imperial Court of Vienna.

♦ **THE INNOVATOR**
Christoph Willibald von Gluck (1714–1787), German composer. He completely reformed the opera.

♦ **THE YOUNG BACH**
Johann Christian Bach (1735–1782), German musician, son of Johann Sebastian. He revitalized instrumental music.

THE APPRENTICESHIP

During the eighteenth century, young people could pursue their musical studies only with the help of private tutors or in religious institutions. Musicians handed down their profession from father to son with strict and demanding training.

Generally, composers were capable of playing several instruments as well as conducting the chorus and the orchestra. A child prodigy is someone who is gifted from birth with natural talent. It is the teacher's responsibility to train the student through rigorous exercises. Talent alone is not enough; to learn the language and rules of composing, the child needs a teacher at his or her side. Mozart happened to have a father who was both a teacher and a musician. Once Leopold recognized his son's virtuosity, he devoted the rest of his life to the education and success of his son.

♦ **THE FATHER**
Leopold Mozart (above, in a portrait attributed to Pietro Antonio Lorenzoni) was born in Augsburg in 1719. His father was a bookbinder. For his earlier musical studies, he attended the town's Jesuit school. He then moved to Salzburg to study philosophy and law at the university, but gave that up in favor of his enduring passion for music. He served first under the Count Thurn und Taxis, and then, under the Archbishop of Salzburg as a violin teacher in 1744, Vice Court Conductor (Vice-Kapellmeister) in 1763, and piano teacher in 1777, but he soon began to concentrate on his son's career. In time, however, their relationship deteriorated, as Wolfgang no longer tolerated his authority. When Leopold died in 1787, father and son were almost strangers.

♦ **LEOPOLD'S TREATISE ON VIOLIN PLAYING**
In 1756, when Wolfgang was born, Leopold Mozart became famous after the publication of his method for violin study. His book was used for years by violin teachers.

♦ **NANNERL**
Mozart's sister, Maria Anna, called Nannerl, was five years older than Wolfgang. She too was a very precocious child with a talent for the harpsichord, but not composition. In time, her relationship with her brother grew cold. Married to Baron Berchtold zu Sonnenburg, she died in London in 1829.

MOZART'S LIFE

1. ♦ *Wolfgang Amadeus Mozart was born in Salzburg on January 27, 1756 to Leopold, a musician in the service of the Archbishop of Salzburg, and Anna Maria Pertl. The family was not rich, but Leopold's good professional reputation guaranteed a comfortable life for the Mozarts. Around 1760 Wolfgang began to learn the harpsichord, violin, and composition. Between five and six years, he mastered the* solfeggio *(musical scales) and the first elements of musical theory, and was ready to perform in public. He composed his first works at the end of 1761. In January, 1762, with his father and sister, he left on his first trip to Munich for the court of the Prince Elector Maximilian.* ➣

♦ **THE MOTHER**
Anna Maria Pertl, born in 1720, died in 1778 in Paris while accompanying her son on one of his tours.

♦ **THE FRIEND**
Johann Andreas Schachtner, court trumpeter for the Archbishop of Salzburg, and Leopold's friend, witnessed the first creations of the extraordinarily talented young Mozart.

♦ **FATHER AND SON**
Under Leopold's vigilant guidance, Wolfgang learned to recognize notes on the staff, to subdivide the tempo, and to execute his first composition exercises even before he could read and write.

THE FIRST STEP
At the end of 1761, Mozart was already a composer. His first minuet, a charming piece, is one of the pieces that children still learn today when they begin to study the piano.

The Child Prodigy

It is a common belief that precocity is a distinctive sign of great musical talent. In the eighteenth century, particularly gifted children performed before courts and in royal palaces. A child prodigy is expected to possess such skills as memory, technical virtuosity, and physical endurance, which have little to do with a typical composer's skills. Above all, a prodigy has to amaze. From this, he or she acquires the habit of facing the public to build confidence in his or her art. Mozart is the most famous child prodigy in the history of music. At age seven, he performed with great success in front of Empress Maria Theresa.

♦ **The European courts**
In 1762, when Mozart played in front of Maria Theresa of Austria (above, in a portrait by Martin van Maytens), a wave of reform policies had swept the European courts. Some regents, such as the same Maria Theresa (1740–1780), Frederick II of Prussia (1740–1786), and Catherine II of Russia (1762–1796), due to the pressure exerted by the emerging social classes and the spread of new ideas during the Age of Reason, approved important reforms to the organization of the state. Maria Theresa and, later, her son, Joseph II, who succeeded her in 1780, modernized the bureaucracy, promoted schooling, extended fiscal obligations to nobles and clergy, and took a fresh interest in music.

Schönbrunn
The summer residence of the Hapsburgs, Schönbrunn Castle, with its immense park, lies just outside Vienna. It was completed in 1749, as ordered by Maria Theresa.

♦ **His father's presence**
Leopold was always present at his son's performances, which were an opportunity for him to meet with nobles and to increase his family's income.

♦ **The successor**
Joseph, Maria Theresa's son, became co-regent with his mother in 1765.

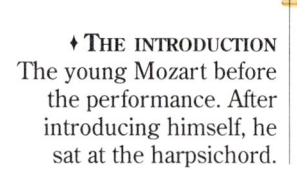

2. Mozart's Life ♦ *In October, 1762, the Mozarts were received in Schönbrunn where Wolfgang played for the imperial court. The following year Leopold organized an exhausting trip to the courts of Europe, a trip that took him to Munich, Augsburg, Schwetzingen (where he had the opportunity to listen to one of the most famous orchestras of the time, that of Mannheim), Heidelberg, Mainz (where he played in front of the young Goethe), Bonn, Cologne, Aachen, Brussels, Paris, and other cities. In 1764 Wolfgang went to London, where he met Johann Christian Bach, and, later, to Holland. At the end of 1765, exhausted by the constant traveling, he became very ill.* ➤

♦ **The introduction**
The young Mozart before the performance. After introducing himself, he sat at the harpsichord.

♦ **THE PARK**
Construction was in progress in Schönbrunn's 296-acre (120 hectare) gardens.

♦ **THE DUCHESS**
Isabel of Parma, Maria Theresa's daughter-in-law. She married Prince Joseph in 1760.

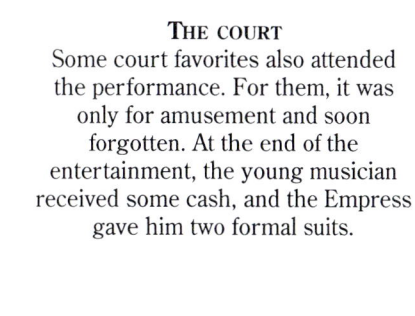

THE COURT
Some court favorites also attended the performance. For them, it was only for amusement and soon forgotten. At the end of the entertainment, the young musician received some cash, and the Empress gave him two formal suits.

♦ **THE YOUNG PRODIGIES**
In the history of music, there are several cases of remarkably gifted children. Their performances were aimed at astonishing the audience with tricks similar to the performances of jugglers. Someone once challenged Mozart, who, during these occasions, always performed some of his own compositions, to sit at a harpsichord that was covered with a cloth spread over the keys and play! In the spring of 1770, in Florence, Mozart became friendly with a talented young violinist, the Englishman Thomas Linley, who was his age. Linley died in 1778 at only 22 years old. Even Ludwig van Beethoven's (1770–1827) father asked his son to perform in public to show the precocity of his son's talent, lying about the real age of his child. Above, a portrait of Beethoven as a young man.

♦ **MARIE ANTOINETTE**
The little Marie Antoinette, Maria Theresa's daughter and future Queen of France, was also in the audience. She was guillotined during the French Revolution.

♦ **THE EMPRESS**
Maria Theresa showed interest in the young Mozart. He had been invited to the court by her son Joseph, who had previously listened to one of his concerts in Vienna.

SALZBURG

The musical climate of the town where Mozart took his first steps as a composer was permeated by the presence of an ecclesiastical court under the sovereignty of Archbishop Hieronymus von Colloredo. Composers were obliged to satisfy the clergy's requests to accompany rites and religious ceremonies, essentially masses, church sonatas, cantatas, oratorios, offertories, and motets. Musicians who worked in a small town for an ecclesiastical institution had to be resigned to operate within a very limited creative circle. They received no commissions for theatrical operas or instrumental music and lived on their own salary. As soon as he could, Mozart left Salzburg to move to a much more stimulating town: Vienna.

♦ **THE CITY**
In Mozart's time, Salzburg, at the northern side of Austria, was the capital of a small principality. Its population was less than 10,000.

♦ **THE PALACE**
The Archbishop's court, which dominated the town's religious and musical life, was situated in the large palace in Salzburg's main square. Music lessons were given inside the palace. Leopold and Wolfgang alternated as teachers, but, actually, Wolfgang disliked teaching.

THE PERFORMERS
Performers for a mass by Mozart in 1773. Wind instruments, organ, timpani, and strings are present, as well as a 28-member choir for four voices: sopranos, tenors, contraltos, and basses.

1 TIMPANI
1 ORGANIST
2 OBOES
4 TRUMPETS

♦ **THE CATHEDRAL**
Built in the seventeenth century in the baroque style, it was the center of city life.

♦ **MUSICAL SITES**
Salzburg did not have an opera house. Some musical dramas were performed at the court of the Archbishop or at the university. Even those who were familiar with symphonies and serenades made up only a small group. The larger public listened to sacred music, especially that performed in the cathedral (above, in an engraving by Kurt Remshard).

♦ **THE ARCHBISHOP**
Hieronymus, Count of Colloredo (1732–1812), Archbishop of Salzburg beginning in 1772, in a portrait by Johann Michael Greiter. His relationship with Mozart was always very tense, and ended abruptly.

21 ADULT CHOIR SINGERS
7 CHOIRBOYS
6 FIRST VIOLINS
6 SECOND VIOLINS
4 VIOLAS
3 CELLOS
2 DOUBLE BASSES

THE COMPOSITION
Mozart composed the *Missa in honorem Sanctissimae Trinitatis* (Mass in Honor of the Holy Trinity) in 1773 for the Archbishop of Salzburg.

3. MOZART'S LIFE ♦ *In 1766 Mozart traveled again, this time to Holland, then to Paris, where he composed his first sacred opera. The long trip back home to Salzburg, via France and Switzerland, ended in November. In 1767, in Salzburg, he studied composition under his father's guidance. He then fled to Olmütz to try to avoid a smallpox epidemic, but he still contracted the disease. At the end of the year, after a stay in Brünn, he returned to Vienna.* ⇒

11

The Italian Musical Environment

During the eighteenth century, the Italian musical environment was among the most prestigious in Europe and attracted young musicians from everywhere who were eager to complete their training. Any musical form, from the serious to the comic opera, from instrumental to vocal music, had its celebrated protagonists in Italy, and Italian musicians occupied dominant positions in the musical life of various courts. Padre Martini's *Accademia Filarmonica* in Bologna was the most distinguished teaching center. Mozart studied counterpoint there.

♦ **Italian music**
In the eighteenth century, Italy was host to a wide variety of musical environments: big operatic production centers like Milan and Naples, capitals of instrumental music, and Venice, home of the violin schools. Many Italian musicians held important positions in European musical centers and courts: Salieri and Tretta were in Vienna, Paisiello and Cimarosa in Petersburg, Clementi in London, and Scarlatti in Lisbon. Above, Padre Martini.

♦ **Antono Caldara** (1670–1736)

♦ **Johann Christian Bach** (1735–1782)

♦ **Camillo Zanotti** (1545–1591)

♦ **Alessandro Scarlatti** (1660–1725)

♦ **Giuseppe Sammartini** (1693–1751)

♦ **Georg Friedrich Händel** (1685–1759)

♦ **Antonio Vivaldi** (1678–1742)

♦ **Padre Martini** (1704–1784) He was both a physicist and a mathematician and had many pupils, including Johann Christian Bach. He collected an extensive musical library and published a remarkable treatise on counterpoint.

♦ **CARLO FARINELLI**
(1705–1782)

♦ **ARCANGELO CORELLI**
(1653–1713)

THE GALLERY
Padre Martini collected the portraits of the musicians he met. Some artists left them as gifts; others were asked to pose.

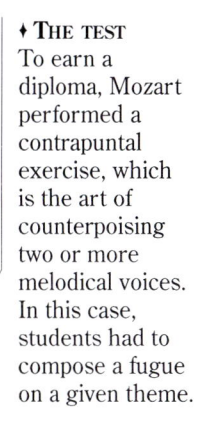

♦ **THE REWARD**
In Rome in July, 1770, Mozart was honored by Pope Clement XIV with the Cross of the Order of the Golden Spur, shown in this later painting.

♦ **THE TEST**
To earn a diploma, Mozart performed a contrapuntal exercise, which is the art of counterpoising two or more melodical voices. In this case, students had to compose a fugue on a given theme.

♦ **THE DIPLOMA**
The diploma, is the certificate that conferred the title of *Accademico* of Bologna on the 15-year-old Mozart. The test was held in the library of the *Accademia Filarmonica*, on January 5, 1771.

4. MOZART'S LIFE ♦ *Early in 1769 Mozart was once again in Salzburg, where he was promoted to the position of* Conzertmeister *of the Archbishop's court. In December his first trip to Italy with his father began. In 1770 he was in Verona, Milan (where* Mitridate, rè di Ponto [Mithridates, King of Pontus] *was performed), Mantua, Florence, and Rome. In Bologna, he was awarded the certificate of* Accademico. *Then, in March 1771 he headed back to Salzburg. A second trip to Italy ended in December when Archbishop Sigismund von Schrattenbach died.* ⇒

From Harpsichord to Piano

In the last decades of the eighteenth century, there was a great evolution in keyboard instruments. This was due to the development of a mechanism that allowed the performer to obtain sounds of different intensity by varying the pressure on the key. For the harpsichord, different pressures on the key make no difference in sound intensity. On the other hand, the fortepiano and the piano allow one to play, as their names suggest, *piano* and *forte* (soft and loud), attaining a much wider variety of effects. This revolution renewed musical writing and the role of the instrumentalist.

♦ **THE KEYBOARD INSTRUMENTS**
Compared to the wind and string instruments, keyboard instruments have greater versatility. They can produce different notes simultaneously and are polyphonic, suitable for either accompaniment or solo performances. Besides the harpsichord, the virginal, the clavichord, and the spinet (above) have been on the musical scene for centuries.

♦ **BARTOLOMEO CRISTOFORI**
Cristofori (1655–1731), who worked in Florence at the Medicean court, is considered the inventor of the modern piano. His first model dates from 1709.

♦ **RUCKERS' HARPSICHORDS**
The Flemish Hans Ruckers (c.1550–c.1625) was a celebrated harpsichord maker. Only 25 of his instruments have survived.

♦ **PLUCKED STRINGS, STRUCK STRINGS**
The harpsichord, the virginal (above), and the spinet are plucked-string keyboard instruments; their sound volumes remain unchanged, no matter how hard the string is plucked. The clavichord, the fortepiano, and the piano are struck-string keyboard instruments; their sound volumes increase when the pressure on the key is stronger.

♦ **ONE-MANUAL HARPSICHORD**
The majority of harpsichords had only one manual.

♦ **TWO-MANUAL HARPSICHORD**
Two manuals or keyboards give different sounds.

♦ **THE MECHANISM OF THE CLAVICHORD**
The small pole that swings on a pin has a metallic element, called a tangent, which, from the inside of the case, strikes the string from below.

♦ **THE CHAMBER CONCERT**
A clavichord concert with strings and winds, by G. Schüler.

♦ **THE MECHANISM OF THE HARPSICHORD**
The string is plucked by a plectrum, or pick, mounted on a small wooden pole, called a jack, which is forced by the key to do a down-up movement.

♦ **THE PIANO MECHANISM**
The hammer strikes the string and then falls backwards, leaving the string to vibrate until the key is released.

♦ **THE PIANO EVOLUTION**
The perfection of the piano has taken time. The evolution went from the attachment of the pedals (around 1770), to the extension of the keyboard's range—from four to seven octaves—to the manufacturing of upright models (in the early XIX century), to the fusion of the frame into a single piece (1872), to the continuous improvements of the mechanism. Since the end of the XIX century, there have been no improvements. Above, a modern piano.

♦ **CRISTOFORI'S INSTRUMENT**
One of the two existing fortepiani by Cristofori.

♦ **IN MOZART'S TIME**
A harpsichord built between 1780 and 1790, similar to those available in Mozart's time. The extension is limited to four and a half octaves.

15

MUSICIANS AND MUSIC PUBLISHERS

During the eighteenth century, a more widespread application of copperplate engraving, known for more than a century, promoted the development of music publishing establishments with whom Mozart's father had contacts. The many European publishing houses prospered, thanks to a larger audience, made up of educated nobles and sophisticated bourgeois who were interested in buying musical scores. Musical instruments and private teachers made their entrance together into the palaces; the music publisher, who perceived the tastes of the public, became a buyer.

♦ **THE MUSIC PUBLISHERS** When scores were used by professional musicians during a court performance or a liturgical ceremony, copyists were able to satisfy the demand. Starting around 1750, several publishing houses flourished, such as the one founded in Vienna by Carlo Artaria, (above, in a portrait by J. Kreutzinger) or that of the Torricella's family, of Swiss origin, also in Vienna, or of Huberty in Paris. A great number of Haydn's and Mozart's piano or chamber compositions enjoyed a remarkable circulation, thanks to these publishers. Mozart was especially connected to Artaria & Co., who published several of his symphonies, quartets, piano and violin sonatas. Several symphonies and quartets by Haydn were published by Huberty.

♦ **ARTARIA & CO.** The premises of Artaria & Co. in Vienna in a 1786 engraving. Artaria & Co. was the most important music publisher in Vienna and one of the most famous in Europe.

♦ **THE BINDER** Franz Alois Mozart, Leopold's brother, lived in Augsburg, where he worked as a bookbinder.

♦ **THE PRINTER** Johann Jakob Lotter received the bound copies of Leopold Mozart's *Versuch ener gründlichen Violinschule* (Treatise on the Fundamental Art of Violin Playing), which was used until the beginning of the XX century.

♦ **THE COPIES** Leopold Mozart's *Violinschule* volumes, bound and ready to be distributed.

5. MOZART'S LIFE ♦ *In March, 1772, Hieronymus Colloredo was elected Archbishop of Salzburg. Mozart was named* Conzertmeister *(concertmaster). In the fall, he returned to Italy and presented his opera* Lucio Silla *in Milan. In 1773 he went to Vienna, where he looked in vain for an appropriate position. Between 1774 and 1777 he worked in Salzburg, but his relationship with Colloredo was deteriorating. In September, 1777, Mozart began a long trip accompanied by his mother. In Augsburg, where he arrived in October at his uncle Franz Alois's house, he spent his time with his cousin Maria Anna Thekla.* ▶

♦ **THE PRESS**
Even at a bookbinder's firm, the press, a publishing machine with a pressure screw, is useful.

♦ **THE BÄSLE**
Wolfgang had a brief but intense relationship with Maria Anna Thekla Mozart (1758–1841), called Bäsle. A mutual sympathy developed between the two young people, possibly innocent and tender love.

♦ **MOZART AND HIS COUSIN**
Mozart plays with his cousin Maria Anna Thekla, nicknamed Bäsle. They first met at Franz Alois' house in Augsburg in October 1777.

THE JOURNEY

Mozart lived in a world that was both much smaller and much bigger that ours—much smaller because whole continents were practically out of reach, and much bigger because traveling from one place to another was more difficult and slower (it was impossible to cover more than 110–120 miles in a day). No other musician in his time toured as much as he did. He traveled by carriage with his family, their baggage, and some musical instruments. In his letters, he often mentioned how weary he was of these long trips.

♦ **COMMUNICATIONS**
Road conditions were extremely poor. Sometimes mountain roads were paved, especially near passes, but for the most part they were merely excavated surfaces. Above, a detail of an eighteenth-century anonymous painting.

EN ROUTE TO PARIS
Mozart at a rest stop during the long trip across Europe. The musician left Salzburg on September 23, 1777, and arrived in Paris on March 23, 1778.

♦ **THE CARRY-ON TRAVEL INSTRUMENTS**
To compose while he traveled, Mozart carried small spinets with him that could be played in the carriage.

♦ **HIS SOJOURNS**
The map of Mozart's principal destinations during the course of his career. It has been estimated that he spent one quarter of his life traveling—exactly ten years, two months, and eight days.

♦ **THE STABLES**
Inns where the passengers could rest, stables to change horses, and places to repair carriages and harnesses were next to rest stops.

♦ **THE CARRIAGE**
Two strong leather strips supported the weight of the interior of the carriage. In this way, it was set apart from the wheel apparatus and bumps did not shake the entire vehicle.

♦ **THE SUSPENSION**
The wheels had mechanisms that softened the vibrations caused by the rough road paving.

THE OPERA WORLD

The eighteenth century is regarded as the Opera Century because a great number of the composers of that period contributed to the popularization of this sublime genre. There are two principal forms of opera: the *opera seria* (serious opera), which depicts memorable historic events, and the *opera comica* (comic opera), which portrays lively sketches of everyday life. The first, which never deals with comic characters, had become artificial and monotonous during Mozart's time, but to distract the audience from the tragic events they represented, the practice of playing *intermezzi buffi* between the acts became popular. Although they were performed during the same evening, the two genres were strictly independent. Mozart, who would write some of his masterpieces for the musical theater, renewed both genres.

♦ **THE *OPERA COMICA* (COMIC OPERA)**
A new genre was born with the *buffi* characters, who were not a part of the *opera seria*—the *opera comica* (comic opera), which gradually increased in importance during the eighteenth century. It was originally performed during intermissions of the *opera seria*, but later became an independent genre. The spontaneity of the subjects permitted very spirited theatrical effects and had important effects on the music, as well, which then followed the action from a closer perspective. The composers of comic operas include: Giovan Battista Pergolesi (1710–1736) in the portrait above, Niccolò Piccinni (1728–1800), Baldassarre Galuppi (1706–1785), Giovanni Paisiello (1740–1816), and Domenico Cimarosa (1749–1801).

♦ **THE INTERMEZZO**
The custom of inserting a short comic piece in the intermissions of the *opera seria* was adopted during the first half of the eighteenth century. A painted backdrop represented the intermezzo.

♦ **LA SERVA PADRONA**
This is the masterpiece *buffo* of Giovan Battista Pergolesi. It tells of the adventures of an old man dominated by his maid, who would end up marrying him.

♦ **UBERTO**
He is a callous old bachelor, rich but weak and hesitant and dominated by the strong personality of his young maid.

♦ **DURING THE INTERMISSION**
During the *intermezzo buffo*, the singers of the *Armida*, by Pasquale Anfossi, prepare to reenter. The subject of the opera is taken from the *Gerusalemme Liberata* by Torquato Tasso.

♦ **THE THEATER**
A view of Turin's *Teatro Regio*, solemnly inaugurated in 1740 with a performance of the *Arsace* with music by Francesco Feo.

♦ **THE *OPERA SERIA* (SERIOUS OPERA)**
During the seventeenth and eighteenth centuries, opera was frequently sung in Italian and was dominated by Italian theorists and composers who codified its form. In the eighteenth century, the Venetian librettist Apostolo Zeno (1668–1750), shown above, dictated the rules of the *opera seria*: Subjects were to be taken from the classics, comic characters were to be completely eliminated, and the scenes were to be grandiose. This brought about splendid scenic creations and allowed the composers to show their talents in pieces of great musical value. However, it also crystallized the performances into rigid forms, far removed from everyday life. The most celebrated composers of serious operas include: Francesco Feo (1691–1761), Niccolò Jommelli (1741–1797), Pasquale Anfossi (1727–1797), and Tommaso Traetta (1727–1779).

♦ **THE CHARACTERS OF THE *OPERA SERIA***
Armida, niece of King Idraote of Damascus, has fallen in love with the crusader Rinaldo. Unfortunately, he does not love her in return, which drives her to suicide.

Paris

In 1778 Mozart was in Paris. During his long stay there, he could not escape the city's great debate between two opera composers—the German Gluck and the Italian Piccinni. The first is the father of an important reform of *opera seria* thanks to his innovations: more musical continuity, singers were forbidden to capriciously embellish their parts, and the chorus had greater importance. In all, the dramatic representation acquired a more unified tone. Mozart, who had always shown great interest in the operatic language, did not participate in the debate, annoying his patron, Baron von Grimm. He remained outside French musical circles and his trip became a disaster, finally ending tragically with his mother's death.

♦ **Gluck and Piccinni**
The German, Christoph Willibald von Gluck (1714–1787), above, in a portrait, arrived in Paris in 1774 on the wave of the enthusiastic receptions in Vienna of his *Orfeo ed Euridice* (1762), *Alceste* (1767), and *Paride ed Elena* (1770). In these works, Gluck discarded the *bel canto* in favor of reproducing the sentiments expressed in the poems (long forgotten in the seventeenth century) and arousing the interest of some of the public. The opposing Italian-influenced wing called Niccolò Piccinni (1728–1800) to Paris in 1776 as its head. Piccinni, a composer with a good comic instinct, but not strong in *opera seria*, found himself involved in a debate that he eventually lost.

♦ **The mother**
Anna Maria Mozart became ill on June 11, 1778 and died on July 3. The cause of her death is unknown.

♦ **The singer**
Giusto Ferdinando Tenducci, (1736–1790), known as the *Senesino* (the small Sienese), *sopranista* and composer—a great Italian singer—was close to Mozart during the days of his mother's illness and after her death.

♦ **The musician**
Johann Christian Bach had already met Mozart many years before in London, in 1764. Bach later moved to Mannheim and then to Paris, where he became a successful opera composer.

♦ **THE SON**
After losing his mother, Mozart was alone in Paris. He was soon forced to leave the city, and unwillingly headed back home.

♦ **THE PARISIAN MUSICAL LIFE**
It was dominated by the Paris Opera House, and two other popular theaters where musical farces, called *vaudevilles*, were performed. In 1752 an Italian comic opera troupe brought the *Serva padrona* by Pergolesi to the stage, contributing to the birth of the national *opera buffa*. Above, a view of Paris.

♦ **THE FRIEND**
Baron Friedrich Melchior von Grimm was one of Mozart's few Parisian patrons. A supporter of Gluck's ideas, he disapproved of the indifference shown by Mozart toward the musical controversy.

6. MOZART'S LIFE ♦ *He left Augsburg at the end of October, 1777, and remained in Mannheim for four months, where he encountered the court musicians. He listened to the celebrated town orchestra and met and fell in love with Aloysia Weber. In March, 1778, he was in Paris, where he composed many of his instrumental operas (symphonies, concertos, and sonatas), performed concertos, and gave private lessons. However, he failed to break into the Parisian world of opera and find an appointment. On July 3, his mother died after a brief illness. At the end of September, he gave in to Leopold's wishes, who considered the entire stay a disaster, and fled Paris.*

Haydn

A composer who served an aristocratic family was able to enjoy several advantages: job security, economic stability, a certain amount of independence, and the ability to experiment with different musical genres. Such was the case with Franz Joseph Haydn, who for at least 50 years composed music for the rich and noble family of Esterházy. In their splendid Hungarian residence, complete with a chapel, a theater, and a spacious concert room, he was able to display his true talent. Haydn's greatest contribution is chamber music and symphonies. He is considered the father of the modern symphony and the first eminent composer of trios and quartets.

♦ **Haydn**
Born in Rohrau in 1732, he went to St. Stephen's Cathedral in Vienna when he was eight years old to be a choirboy. He received his musical training in the Austrian capital and, in 1761, was employed by the Esterházy family (first by Prince Paul Anton, then, by his brother Nicolaus), spending long periods of time in the residence of Esterház, in modern Hungary. Here, the princes, who were passionate music lovers, lived in opulence. Upon Nicolaus' death, Haydn moved to London. Later, he returned to Vienna, where he died in 1809. His artistic production is extraordinary in quality and quantity: more than 100 symphonies, 83 quartets for strings, 52 piano sonatas, 31 trios, operas, sacred music, cantatas, and intermezzi. He knew Mozart, and Beethoven was one of his students. He is considered the first distinguished master of musical classicism.

The residence
Its construction began in 1762 as a project of the architect Johannes Ferdinand Mödlhammer. It ended in 1784. It was a summer residence for the princes. In winter, they lived not too far away in Eisenstadt Castle.

♦ **INSIDE THE RESIDENCE** Receptions were held in the gala room. In Esterház, there was also an opera theater, inaugurated in 1768, a library, a picture gallery, a puppet theater, a collection of mirrors and another of clocks, a rose garden, a zoo, and an immense park. The property was protected by an army of 150 grenadiers.

♦ **THE IMPRESARIO** Johann Peter Salomon (1745–1815), German composer and violin player. He moved to London in 1781, where he welcomed Haydn and commissioned from him the oratorio *The Creation* and a famous set of symphonies, the last 12 composed by the Austrian musician.

♦ **THE INSTRUCTIONS** Every day Haydn had to communicate the prince's request for the music for that day to the 15 musicians under his authority.

♦ **THE PRINCE** Nicolaus Esterházy (1714–1790), called The Magnificent, was a modest amateur musician and a generous music patron. He gave an annual salary of 400 florins to Haydn and a contract renewable every three years.

7. MOZART'S LIFE ♦ *During his long and exhausting trip back home from Paris, Mozart stopped in Nancy, Salzburg, and Mannheim. He arrived in Munich on Christmas Day, 1778 and stayed at the Weber's house. Aloysia Weber, a singer who was already well known in Munich, refused his marriage proposal. In January, 1779, the composer was once again in Salzburg, where he performed his duties as concertmaster and court organist in the service of the Archbishop. In the meantime, he studied Haydn's compositions, especially the quartets, and composed the* Missa *in C major, K.317, and the* Sinfonia Concertante *for violin and viola, K.364.* ➩

THE MODERN ORCHESTRA

To perform a symphony by Mozart or Haydn, one needs an orchestra that is different from the type that was popular during the first half of the eighteenth century. The differences are the number of the instrumentalists, which grew considerably until it surpassed 30 elements, and the role of the woodwinds, which became more important. Most of all, Mozart and Haydn's orchestra was no longer a group of soloists, but a compact and disciplined ensemble, capable of reaching the volume necessary for a large concert room. Because of the increased number of instrumentalists, a skilled leader was needed to unite the group; thus, the conductor was born.

◆ **WOODWINDS**
Wind instruments without reeds made their appearance in the orchestra during the second half of the eighteenth century. They were appreciated for their versatility and uniform sound.

◆ **OBOES**
A part of the orchestra since the end of the seventeenth century, these are double-reed instruments with a slightly nasal tone, suitable for melodic phrases.

◆ **FIRST VIOLINS**
The first violins play an essential role in the orchestra. The most difficult themes are often given to them. Gradually, the first violin on the left sets the tempo for all the other musicians. The modern role of the orchestra director began with the specialization of the first violin. He or she ensures the ensemble's unity for compositions that have become increasingly complex.

◆ **SECOND VIOLINS**
They play on a lower register than the first violins and not as much skill is required to play them.

♦ **TIMPANI (KETTLEDRUM)**
The only percussive instrument in the eighteenth-century orchestra.

♦ **BASSOONS**
The bassoon is a double-reed instrument whose register is similar to that of the cello. It has occupied a permanent place in the orchestra since the eighteenth century.

♦ **HORNS**
Very ancient instruments, horns were introduced into the orchestra during the eighteenth century. Their resonance, warm and vibrating, is capable of blending the more ethnic sounds.

♦ **TRUMPETS**
These are instruments with a brass mouthpiece. In the eighteenth century, trumpets still had to be perfected and were not able to produce all the notes. Their role was limited to the full resonance of the orchestra when their shrill sound could be heard.

♦ **VIOLAS**
Older than the violins, their role has changed over time. Their sound is lower, somewhat muted, but rich and penetrating. They are placed in the middle of the orchestra. Their warm tone gives a crucial blending of sound to the string section.

♦ **CELLOS**
Tuned an octave below the viola, cellos have the function of harmonic support for the composition's highest sound. In Mozart and Haydn's symphonies, they began to assume a more important role and to impose their warm and low sound in brief solo pieces.

♦ **DOUBLE BASSES**
Introduced in the XVII century, the lowest tone of all the string instruments, used for cello doubling or intensifying, and very seldom had solo parts.

How a Theater Works

In Munich, where *Idomeneo* was premiered, Mozart had a theater with extraordinary possibilities at his disposal. Unlike small town theaters, the Munich Court Theater was equipped with sophisticated machinery for scenery changes and special effects. It had plenty of room for the stage and the orchestra, and it allowed the composer to rehearse until he was sure of the final results. The technical resources that the big theaters started to exhibit toward the end of the eighteenth century encouraged the composers to try scenic and musical innovations, and promoted changes in the tastes of the public, who began to expect increasingly complex shows.

♦ **IDOMENEO**
With this work, Mozart renewed a genre that had remained unchanged and codified for years: the *opera seria*. The libretto (above, title page of the original) by the priest Varesco, narrates the story of Idomeneo, king of Crete. To escape a storm caused by a sea monster, Idomeneo promises Neptune to sacrifice the first person he meets upon his arrival. This person will be his son, Idamante. At the end, Idomeneo will save his son, but he will have to abdicate in his favor. Mozart's music underlines the story with a completely new theatrical perspective: arias, choruses, and concertatos stress the psychology of characters who are moved by subjective feelings. For the first time, an *opera seria* reached the spontaneity and expression that was until then typical only of the *opera comica*.

♦ **THE MONSTER**
The scene of the storm that marks the beginning of the opera "action" required the presence of a sea monster that was made with a frame covered with painted cloths.

♦ **THE BACKDROP**
The sea and the island of Crete were painted on a curtain placed at the end of the stage.

♦ **THE STAGEHANDS**
Their work was hidden from the public. They simulated waves by moving the curtains with a system of pulleys.

8. MOZART'S LIFE ♦ *Mozart spent 1780 between musical engagements and love's disillusions. His opera,* La finta giardiniera, (The Pretend Gardener), *was performed in Augsburg. He composed the* Symphony in C major, K.338, *the* Vesperae solennes de confessore, *K.339, and was involved in a series of court concerts. At the end of October, Aloysia Weber married the actor Joseph Lange. On November 5, Mozart went to Munich where he had been requested to compose a new opera and where the news of the death of Empress Maria Theresa reached him. After three months of rehearsals,* Idomeneo *was finally acclaimed by the public on January 29, 1781.* ➢

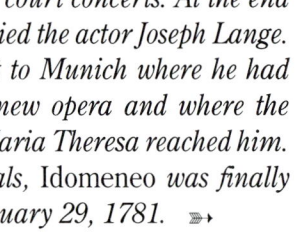

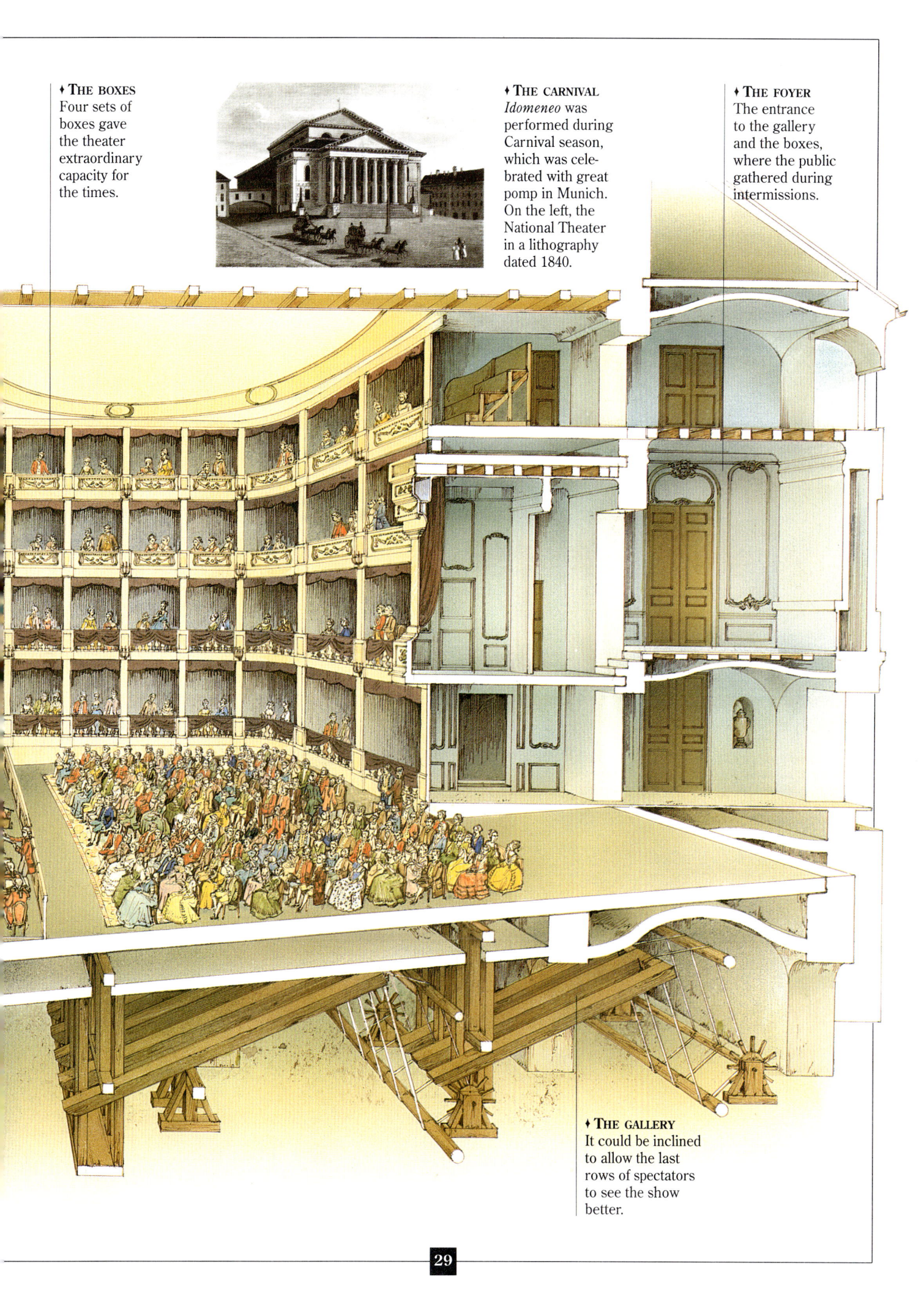

♦ **THE BOXES**
Four sets of boxes gave the theater extraordinary capacity for the times.

♦ **THE CARNIVAL**
Idomeneo was performed during Carnival season, which was celebrated with great pomp in Munich. On the left, the National Theater in a lithography dated 1840.

♦ **THE FOYER**
The entrance to the gallery and the boxes, where the public gathered during intermissions.

♦ **THE GALLERY**
It could be inclined to allow the last rows of spectators to see the show better.

VIENNA

When Mozart arrived in Vienna, it was the European music capital due to private patronage, parties, and a public that was eager to pay to listen to operas and concerts. Viennese musical life, however, depended upon the court. Mozart was determined to win the favor of those in charge of the musical events: Count Orsini-Rosenberg, Antonio Salieri, and Gottlieb Stephanie. He hoped that they would help him win the favor of Emperor Joseph II.

♦ **VIENNA'S MUSICAL LIFE**
In Vienna, there were two imperial theater/opera houses, the *Kärntnerthortheater* and the *Burgtheater* (below, as it looks today), later called the German National Theater, where prose works and lyrical operas were performed. Two distinguished music publishers, Torricella and Artaria & Co., were there, as well as important piano makers Johann and Wenzel Schantz and Anton Walter (above), and concert music associations like the *Tonkünstler-Societät* that had an orchestra of 180 performers. During Lent, academies held musical evening events at which the private orchestras of rich aristocrats performed. A solid tradition of sacred music had existed there for centuries.

♦ **THE CHURCH**
The *Michaelerkirche* (St. Michael's Church) was the one favored by aristocrats and rich landowners who were among society's highest ranks.

♦ **HAYDN'S HOME**
In addition to St. Michael's Church, this was one of the many houses in which the musician lived while in Vienna.

♦ **THE RICH**
During the holidays, the Michaelerplatz was the meeting point of the Viennese high society.

9. MOZART'S LIFE ♦ *After the performance in Munich of* Idomeneo, *instead of going home to Salzburg, Mozart went to Vienna, where the Archbishop under whom he still served, was staying. He took a room at the Weber's residence. He soon became angry at the Archbishop, breaking off their relationship on May 10, 1781. Meanwhile, because of the scheming of Cäcilia Weber, who was looking for a husband for her daughter, Wolfgang started courting Constanze. In Vienna, he began his freelance career as an artist with private lessons and teaching at music schools. The first months spent in the Austrian capital were to be among the happiest of his life.*

♦ **THE CITY**
During the second half of the eighteenth century, Vienna (above, in a view by Bellotto) was, with Naples and Paris, among the largest towns in Europe. It had almost 200,000 inhabitants.

♦ **THE IMPERIAL PALACE**
The *Hofburg*, a modest building from the outside, was the imperial residence.

♦ **THE SCHOOL**
Next to the Burgtheater is the Spanish Riding School, with its famous trained white horses, the Lippizaner.

♦ **THE BURGTHEATER**
Renamed the German National Theater according to Joseph II's order in 1778, it first hosted prose works, then, lyrical operas, but only in German. After 1783, it featured the Italian opera. *Le nozze di Figaro* (The Marriage of Figaro) premiered here.

♦ **THE INSTITUTIONS**
Joseph II with the principal figure on the musical scene: Count Orsini-Rosenberg, the court opera director; Antonio Salieri, *Kapellmeister* (Choirmaster); and Gottlieb Stephanie, Burgtheater's artistic director.

"Turkomania"

Vienna had been besieged by Turkish troops in 1683, and Turkish influences began to be felt among the more educated classes. The contact with distant lands had aroused the curiosity of the Viennese, simultaneously offering them a reassuring way to reassert the superiority of their civilization and to neutralize their fears of losing their identity. "Turkomania" was one of the most curious European fashion trends of the end of the eighteenth century. It can even be found in the field of music, with the flourishing of comic operatic subjects that also appealed to Mozart. A "Turkish"-inspired composition, *Die Entführung aus dem Serail (The Abduction from the Seraglio)* was his first masterpiece in the *opera buffa* genre.

THE FREYUNG
This is a huge irregularly shaped square, not far from downtown Vienna, a theater of popular feasts and a place of torture for convicts sentenced to death.

THE MENACE
In 1683 when Turkish troops besieged Vienna, Count von Starhemberg valiantly overthrew them. At the same time, an imperial army, at the orders of Charles V of Lorraine, defeated the Turks at Kahlenberg.

10. MOZART'S LIFE ♦ *In 1781 Joseph II issued the first reforms, including the Edict of Tolerance which abolished serfdom and authorized religious freedom. During the first months of 1782 Mozart composed* The Abduction from the Seraglio, *which was staged on July 16. On August 4 he married Constanze Weber against his father's wishes. After the marriage, the Mozarts lived a costly lifestyle, but the future seemed promising since Mozart was among the most acclaimed musicians in Vienna. His academy at the Burgtheater performed for the Emperor in March 1783, and was the musical event of the year.* ➤

♦ **A VIEW OF THE SIEGE**
A great number of paintings like this by Franz Gefels, today at the *Historisches Museum der Stadt*, kept the memory of the Turkish menace alive.

♦ **THE CHURCH**
Schottenkirche was built in the baroque style with a bulb-shaped bell tower.

♦ **RUGS**
Oriental rugs and other goods made their appearance in Vienna through frequent contacts with the Ottoman world. They were very expensive and in great demand by noble families.

THE MARKET
In Freyung's square, a fair of oriental objects, brass artifacts, and fabrics was held.

♦ **CLOTHING**
Oriental fabrics and clothing were commonly sold in the Viennese markets.

♦ **THE ABDUCTION FROM THE SERAGLIO**
Premiered in 1782, *The Abduction from the Seraglio* (above, playbill of the first performance) is the composer's first masterpiece in the genre of the *Singspiel*, that form of musical theater where sung parts alternate with spoken dialogues, a model for the *opera comica* in German. It tells the story of the noble Spaniard, Belmonte, in search of his beloved Constanza who has been kidnapped by the pasha Selim. Rejected by the woman, the Turk will prove to be a forgiving man by giving her back to Belmonte. The author of the libretto is Gottlieb Stephanie (1741–1800), who had reviewed a previous work, *Belmonte e Costanza* by Friedrich Bretner (1748–1807).

33

The Entertainment

Music, as a background for festive occasions, recreation, and moments of everyday life, was heard at court, public events, and in the homes of noble families. Short compositions, often performed by woodwinds, accompanied private ceremonies, celebrations, and banquets. Even Mozart and Haydn wrote several entertainment pieces on commission that were a good source of income. After the composition of these short pieces, Mozart assigned a more important role to the winds, changing the entire orchestral language.

♦ **At the prater**
This district of Vienna, on the east side, housed a large public park that attracted many visitors, especially on holidays.

♦ **The Wind Band**
The practice of composing music for small wind bands was typical of Bohemian musicians and soon arrived in Vienna. Generally, it was an octet formed by pairs of oboes, clarinets, horns, and bassoons, which performed during outdoor gala occasions, events, dinners, and military parades.

THE BELVEDERE
The Belvedere gardens, which offered a breathtaking view of Vienna, were ideal for musical entertainment and leisurely strolls. Outside Vienna, south of the downtown area, they were frequented by aristocrats.

11. MOZART'S LIFE ♦ *On June 17, 1783, Wolfgang's and Constanze's first son was born—Raimund Leopold. At the end of July, Wolfgang went to Salzburg. It was to be the composer's last visit to his hometown. Mozart met Colloredo and saw his father and sister (who did not show much warmth toward Constanze). In the meantime, in Vienna, little Raimund Leopold died on August 19 of an intestinal obstruction. One of Mozart's sacred masterpieces, the* Missa *in C minor (Mass in C minor), K.427, was performed on October 26 in the Benedictine Church of Saint Peter in Salzburg. The day after the performance, Mozart and his wife left for Linz.* ♦

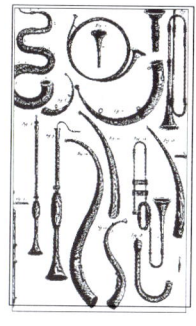

♦ **WOODWINDS**
Different types of woodwinds reproduced in a drawing in the *Encyclopedie* by Diderot and D'Alembert.

♦ **EXERCISES OF STYLE**
The Belvedere was a perfect place in which to sketch or draw the town and its protagonists. There were many views of Vienna executed in the eighteenth century from this site.

CHAMBER MUSIC

The ideal of pure art finds its higher expression in chamber music, a genre that seems to appeal more to the performers than to the listeners. It was not originally meant for a public performance and was not usually heard at celebrations and spectacular engagements. Its more typical form is the string quartet, made up of two violins, a viola, and a cello. Because of the improvement of the instruments, and due to the skillfulness of very talented lutists, this ensemble acquired a superior role and constituted one of the main foundations upon which the new classical language of European musical civilization was based.

♦ **THE INSTRUMENTS**
On the walls, the lutist's tools: saws, hammers, tongs, pincers, and files. On the working desk, glues and varnishes, the quality of which is essential for the sturdiness of the instrument and the purity of the sound.

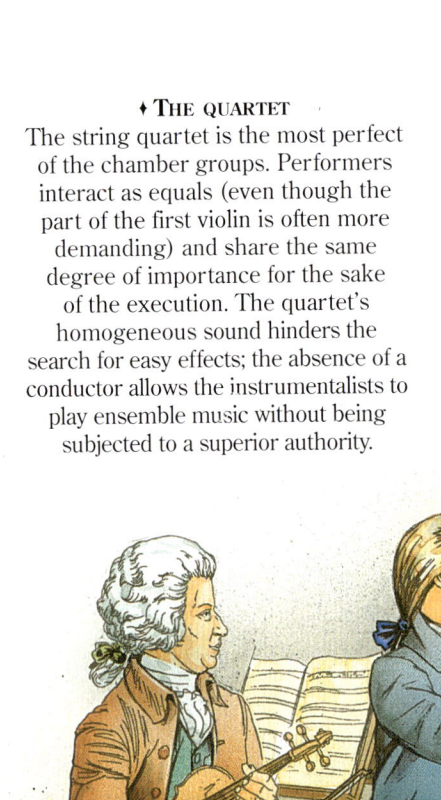

♦ **THE QUARTET**
The string quartet is the most perfect of the chamber groups. Performers interact as equals (even though the part of the first violin is often more demanding) and share the same degree of importance for the sake of the execution. The quartet's homogeneous sound hinders the search for easy effects; the absence of a conductor allows the instrumentalists to play ensemble music without being subjected to a superior authority.

♦ **FOUR GREAT MUSICIANS**
Mozart (viola) performs a quartet together with Haydn (first violin), Vanhal (cello), and Dittersdorf (second violin).

♦ **SCROLL AND FINGERBOARD**
Once the body of the instrument is constructed, a scroll that holds an ebony fingerboard is attached. The strings, tightened by the pegs, are attached to the tailpiece at the base.

♦ **THE DRYING PROCESS**
Once finished, the violin must be hung where it is not too humid, so that the glue used to assemble its components can dry without misshaping the instrument.

♦ **THE GREATEST LUTISTS**
The difficult art of manufacturing string instruments, in particular that of violins, developed in Italy at the beginning of the seventeenth century. The most brilliant lutists were the violin makers of Cremona: Andrea Amati, Giuseppe Guarneri, and above all, Antonio Stradivari (1644–1737), who definitively standardized the instrument's proportions. Although centuries have passed, the instruments made by these master craftsmen are still unparalleled for their sound quality and strong construction. Above, a violin by Guarneri, below a Stradivarius.

♦ **WITHOUT SCREWS**
The mounting of the various parts of the instrument must be done with the minimum possible use of glues and without the use of screws, which could diminish the richenss of its sound.

♦ **THE BOTTOM**
To form the bottom of the instrument, (the part that faces the strings), molds are used from which the shapes are made.

Teaching

Private music lessons began to be a substantial source of income in Mozart's day. Before that time, musicians were trained by their parents or in the courts or religious institutions. Cultivated amateurs, fundamental to a teacher, were sadly missing. The increasing demand for private lessons came from the desire to learn singing or to master an instrument, which was common in every noble and many middle-class houses. During his years in Vienna, Mozart taught constantly and, in some period of his life, teaching represented his only source of income.

♦ **THE STUDENT**
Barbara Ployer was one of Mozart's most gifted pupils. She took piano and composition lessons. Mozart composed the Piano Concerto in E-flat, No. 14, K.449, for her.

♦ **THE FRIEND**
Maria Elisabeth Waldstätten, Mozart's friend during his years in Vienna, contributed to subscription concerts and loaned him some money.

♦ **A NEW HOUSE**
Soon after their marriage, the Mozarts rented a spacious apartment on the High Bridge. Constanze entertained her friends there and Wolfgang taught students.

♦ **ALOYSIA WEBER**
She was one of his students, his sister-in-law, and his unattainable love. The composer gave her singing lessons in Mannheim in 1777.

♦ **FRANZ XAVER SÜSSMAYR**
Mozart's last pupil. He completed Mozart's *Requiem* and set the recitatives of *La Clemenza di Tito (The Clemency of Titus)* to music. Antonio Salieri also instructed him.

♦ **THOMAS ATTWOOD**
An Englishman, he studied composition with Mozart in Vienna between 1785 and 1786. The exercises from the *maestro* that he kept throw some light on Mozart's teaching methods.

♦ **MOZART AS *MAESTRO***
Mozart's execution and theoretical capabilities were incredible. He was able to teach piano, singing, violin, organ, and composition.

12. MOZART'S LIFE ♦ *In Linz, he performed one of his most famous symphonies, Symphony in C, No. 36, the "Linz," K.425. In December 1783 he went to Vienna, and in 1784 he was busy with concerts and academies, and composed chamber music and concertos. On September 21, his second son, Carl Thomas, was born. In December, Mozart became a Freemason. In 1785 his father Leopold visited him. He continued his teaching, taking on new students and starting the composition of* Le nozze di Figaro (The Marriage of Figaro), *on which he was to work during the last months of the year.* ➟

39

THE SONATA FORM

The sonata form is a type of composition born around the mid-eighteenth century, which is based on the presence of two or more themes inside the same piece that are organized in a precise formal scheme. Its main characteristics are: the different character of the themes; their vivacious dialectic—almost an antagonism between opposed principles; and the final statement of the tonality of the first of them, which produces the impression of the piece's victorious conclusion. For its dramatic and, at the same time, rigorously logic character, the sonata form is considered one of the most perfect musical creations. Haydn contributed decisively to its codification. Mozart and, later, Beethoven contributed immensely to its evolution.

EXPOSITION — A

DEVELOPMENT — B

RECAPITULATION — A'

♦ **THE SCHEME**
Its form is based on a triple division of a movement, along the scheme A-B-A'. The first section (A) is called the exposition, the second (B) the development, and the third (A') the recapitulation. In the exposition, the two themes are presented; in the development, they are expanded into new episodes; and in the recapitulation, the material of the exposition is repeated, but with significant modifications.

A

♦ **FIRST THEME**
The beginning of the composition, it gives the whole tonality to the piece.

♦ **MODULATING BRIDGE**
It links the first theme to the second one through a modulating episode.

♦ **SECOND THEME**
It contrasts openly with the first one.

♦ **CODETTA**
It concludes the exposition, which, after the codetta, is repeated with a refrain.

♦ **EXPOSITION**
In the movement's first part, the two themes are heard, linked to a transitional passage that brings a change of tonality. They are the materials that will be used to build the sonata form.

B

♦ **FIRST EPISODE**
It is recalled from the first theme with some modifications.

♦ **SECOND EPISODE**
This is an idea derived from the second theme.

♦ **THIRD EPISODE**
The second theme is traced differently.

♦ **FOURTH EPISODE**
The coda brings the development to its conclusion.

♦ **DEVELOPMENT**
This is the most innovative section of the sonata form. The two themes are heard again. They are now treated more liberally and are accompanied by new episodes.

A'

♦ **FIRST THEME**
It reappears exactly as in the exposition.

♦ **MODULATING BRIDGE**
It links the first theme to the second one, but without changing tonality.

♦ **SECOND THEME**
This time it is presented in the same tonality as the first one.

♦ **FINAL CODA**
It concludes the composition, always in the same tonality.

♦ **RECAPITULATION**
This is the phase when all the material heard during the course of the exposition is repeated. It contains only the elements of the exposition, but is presented in a different way. Now they are exposed in the piece's basic tonality.

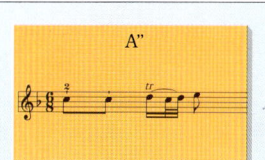

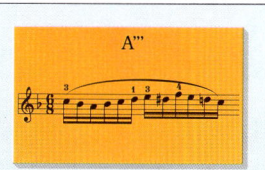

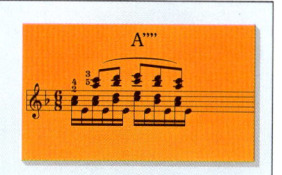

A	A'	A''	A'''	A''''
♦ **THEME** It is presented at the beginning of the piece.	♦ **FIRST VARIATION** It is similar to the theme, only a little faster (*più mosso*).	♦ **SECOND VARIATION** Greater elaboration of the theme.	♦ **THIRD VARIATION** It is developed in a minor tonality.	♦ **FOURTH VARIATION** Only an expert recognizes the theme.

♦ **THEME WITH VARIATIONS** It is often the second movement of a sonata or a symphony; if it is not in a sonata form again, it is a theme with variations. In this form, a theme (often a very simple one) that is exposed at the beginning of the piece is gradually elaborated until it reaches a certain complexity.

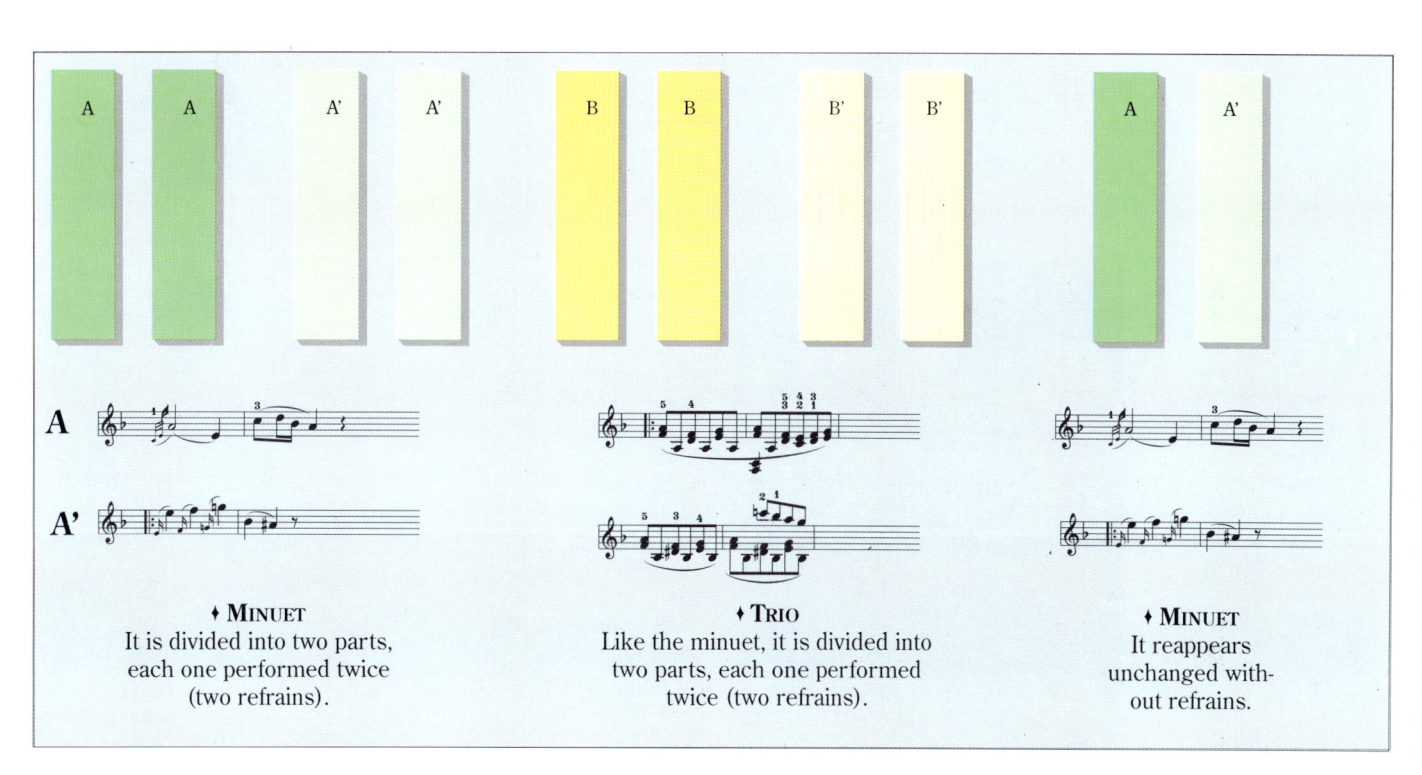

♦ **MINUET** It is divided into two parts, each one performed twice (two refrains).	♦ **TRIO** Like the minuet, it is divided into two parts, each one performed twice (two refrains).	♦ **MINUET** It reappears unchanged without refrains.

♦ **THE MINUET** It is a dance in 3/4 time that originated and was popular in France and was introduced in courts during the seventeenth century. It consists of three sections: the minuet itself with two refrains; a central more extended part, called a trio, because it was originally played by three solo players; and the repetition of the minuet without refrains. It has no coda.

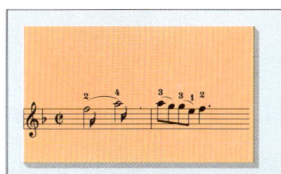

♦ **THEME** It is presented at the beginning of the piece.	♦ **FIRST EPISODE** It has nothing in common with the theme.	♦ **THEME** It is recalled without modifications.	♦ **SECOND EPISODE** It is different from the theme and the first episode.	♦ **THEME** It is without modifications and with a final coda.

♦ **THE RONDO** The last tempo of a composition is often written in this musical form. The rondo is based on a scheme in which the theme is followed by episodes based on completely different materials. When it reappears, it is never substantially modified as in the sonata form.

The Librettists

The librettist writes the text of a work, such as an opera. His or her task is to write verses to be set to music by the composer, often adapting preexisting subjects but always keeping an eye on their compatibility with the needs of the music, which are very different from those of the theater. The operas of the first half of the eighteenth century, particularly of the serious genre, due in part to a lack of good librettists, are frequently of modest overall value. Mozart had the good fortune to find a very fine librettist in the Italian Lorenzo da Ponte. In his work, the theater's needs and the music resources are perfectly balanced, allowing the composer to fully demonstrate his exquisite craftsmanship.

♦ **Lorenzo da Ponte**
The activity of this great Italian librettist of Jewish origin was vital to Mozart's theatrical successes and to the evolution of the *opera buffa*. Born in Ceneda (today, Vittorio Veneto) in 1749, da Ponte converted to Christianity and took sacred orders in 1773. He led an adventurous life and lived in several European countries. His years in Vienna (1781–1791) were the most prolific of his career. Besides the three libretti for Mozart (*Le nozze di Figaro, Don Giovanni*, and *Così fan tutte*, he wrote many other successful ones: for Salieri (*Il ricco di un giorno, Il talismano, Il pastor fido*); for Soler (*Una cosa rara, Il burbero di buon cuore*); and for Martini (*L'arbore di Diana*). In 1819 he moved to the United States, where he died in 1838. His memoirs are a valuable source of information used to reconstruct Vienna during that period.

♦ **Rousseau**
Rousseau (1712–1778) wrote *Le devin du village* (The Village Soothsayer), the basis of one of Mozart's earliest operas, *Bastien und Bastienne*.

♦ **Metastasio**
Italian poet and librettist (1698–1782), he worked for more than 50 years at the Viennese court. His texts were set to music by a countless number of composers.

♦ **Censorship**
All the stage subjects needed approval of a censor. In the case of *The Marriage of Figaro*, da Ponte had pleaded his cause in front of the Emperor himself. Left, a reception in the Redeoutensaal to celebrate the marriage between Archduke Joseph (not yet Emperor) and Isabel of Parma.

13. Mozart's Life ♦ *The beginning of 1786 was devoted to the composition of* Der Schauspieldirektor (The Impresario), *presented at Schönbrunn on February 7, and to the conclusion of* The Marriage of Figaro. *This work of Mozart and Da Ponte was successfully staged at the Burgstheater on May 1. A month earlier, Mozart had taught at his last academy in Vienna. After* The Marriage of Figaro, *he composed such chamber and symphonic pieces as: the* Piano Quartet in E-flat, K.493, *the* String Quartet in D, K.499, *the* Piano Concerto in C, K.503, *and the* Symphony in D, "Prague" K.504. *In October, his third son, Johann Thomas Leopold, was born. He died less than a month later.* ➺

♦ **WIELAND** German poet (1733–1813), author of the fable from which the idea of *Die Zauberflöte* (The Magic Flute) is taken.

♦ **BEAUMARCHAIS** French comedy writer (1732–1799), he performed his own *Figaro* in 1781. The drama was at first banned by King Louis XVI of France.

♦ **MOZART** The composition of *Figaro* took very little time (about six weeks). His relationship with the librettist was very close.

♦ **DA PONTE** He received a proposal from Mozart, whom he met in Vienna, in 1785, to write the libretto of *Figaro*, modeled after the work by Beaumarchais.

The Marriage of Figaro

With this opera, a comedy that perfectly balances joy and sorrow, Mozart and da Ponte brought to the stage the protagonists of the lowest social classes. Figaro, Count Almaviva's barber and valet, is going to marry Susanna, the countess' maid. The Count, who fancies the girl, tries every possible trick to impede the marriage with the help of the conniving Bartolo, Marcellina, and Basilio. His efforts will be fruitless and, in the end, he has to agree to the marriage.

♦ **The history of the opera**
The Marriage of Figaro premiered at the Burgtheater, in Vienna, on May 1, 1786. The work has the structure of an Italian comic opera, with *recitativi secchi* (recitative style), arias, and closed ensemble pieces (*"commedia per musica"* was written on the title page). Its literary source is the comedy *Le mariage de Figaro ou la folle journée* by the French author Pierre Augustin Caron de Beaumarchais (1732–1799), performed in Paris in 1784. The work, which had few rehearsals in Vienna, was a triumph in Prague in the winter of 1787. Above, a portrait by Beaumarchais; below, a detail of a stage sketch: the Count kissing the hand of the Countess.

The scene
The finale of the second act, with almost all the characters on the stage, is a difficult moment for Figaro—the Count and his allies threaten to give him Marcellina for a wife.

♦ **Cherubino**
The youthful Countess' page, interpreted by a feminine voice, brings to the stage the first sounds of adolescent love.

♦ **Mozart**
The composer sits at the harpsichord while he conducts the opera's first performance.

♦ **Figaro and Susanna**
The two lovers live in the Count's palace. Even though they are simple servants, they know how to pursue their goal with intelligence and wit, succeeding in subverting the Count's crafty plans.

♦ **THE COUNT**
Shady and dark, he would like to reestablish the ancient feudal claim, to win Susanna. He will end up begging the Countess's forgiveness.

♦ **BARTOLO**
Remembering a former misdeed by Figaro, he is on the Count's side.

♦ **THE MUSIC**
With *The Marriage of Figaro*, Mozart proved himself able to renew the patterns of the *opera buffa*, ending them in a way that is no longer only comic. He succeeded in adapting those patterns to the dramatic action, and more important, in creating music that explored the characters' feelings while the situation changed. This clearly shows in the ensemble pieces, fantastic for their quality and amplitude, especially during the act finales (that of the second act, in particular). The musical creation follows the libretto narration, adhering to it with a series of completely new solutions. In this way, the music of *The Marriage of Figaro* can be happy or melancholy, lively or meditative, light or dramatic, without ever giving the impression of technical artificiality or lack of feeling. Above, a detail of a stage sketch.

♦ **THE COUNTESS**
A noble and tormented figure, she endures her husband's changeable moods and is on the side of Susanna and Figaro. At the end, she will forgive her husband.

♦ **DON BASILIO**
Music scholar and the Count's jack-of-all-trades, he is the typical scheming individual who plans to destroy the lovers' dreams, not out of personal interest, but because he is evil.

♦ **MARCELLINA**
The elderly woman is in love with Figaro, and she holds an old marriage promise in her hands. An unexpected twist reveals that Figaro is her long-lost son and Bartolo is his father.

45

THE CONCERTO

Until the mid-eighteenth century, a concerto was defined as a composition for a group of instrumentalists, one or more of whom was a soloist (but always within the boundaries of a compact musical fabric) and all the others performed as a group. The use of more sophisticated instruments led to the distinct separation between soloist and group. The soloist (usually, a pianist or violinist) was counterpoised to the orchestra, working with it as an equal, and became the protagonist of the musical presentation. A performer's skills became as important as the quality of the composition. The public came to admire the soloist and was willing to pay to listen to the concerto.

♦ **SUBSCRIPTION CONCERTS**
Organized by the composer and conductor, who collected the funds before the event. This is one of the two tickets left for concerts given by Mozart. It dates from the first years of his time in Vienna.

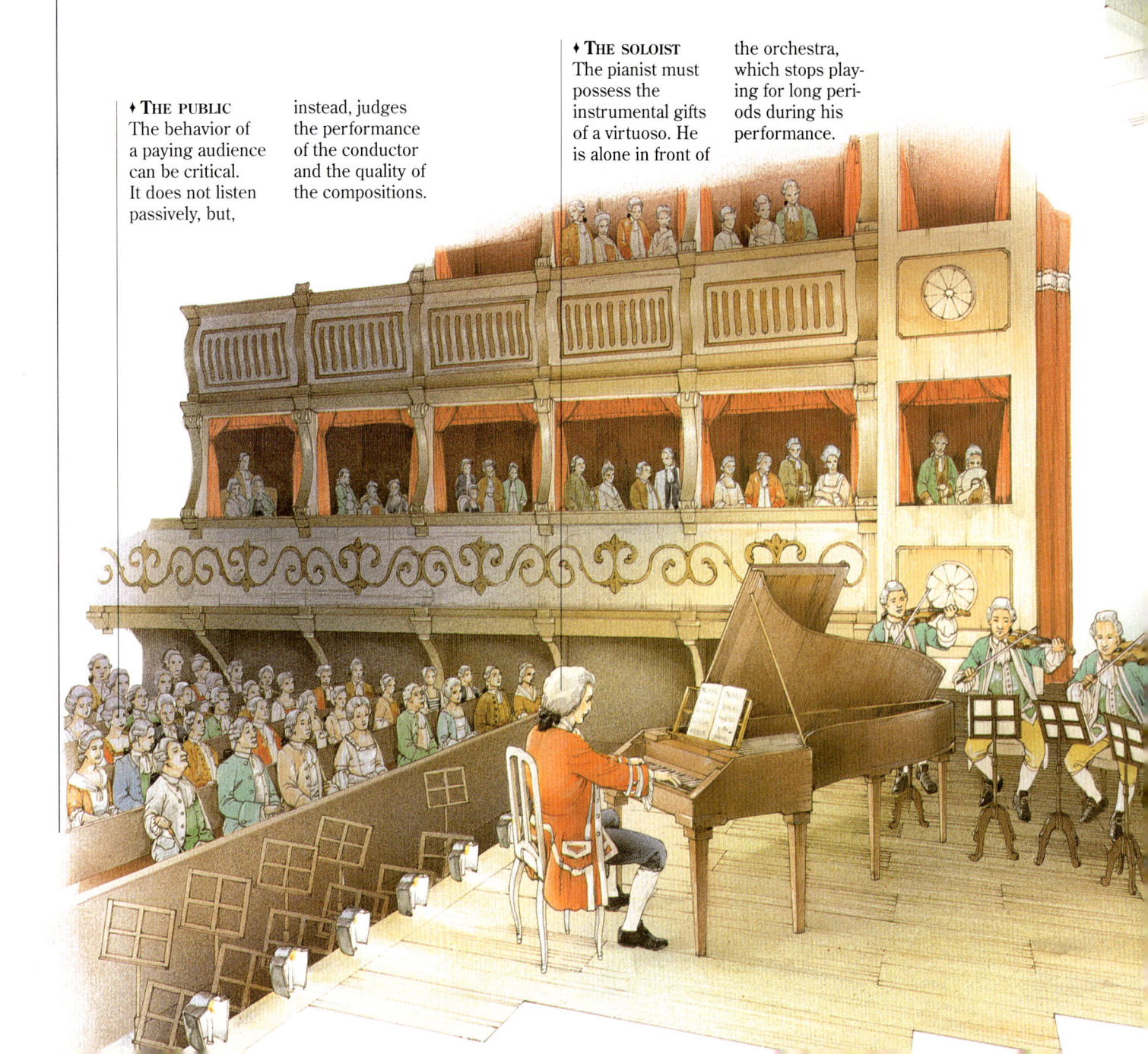

♦ **THE PUBLIC**
The behavior of a paying audience can be critical. It does not listen passively, but, instead, judges the performance of the conductor and the quality of the compositions.

♦ **THE SOLOIST**
The pianist must possess the instrumental gifts of a virtuoso. He is alone in front of the orchestra, which stops playing for long periods during his performance.

♦ **A SOCIAL EVENT** The concert was also a social event. During the intermission, people exchanged their own impressions and had the opportunity to meet new friends outside the restricted circle of the salons.

♦ **THE ORCHESTRA** It alternates with the soloist. Between the soloist and the orchestra, a challenging dialogue begins, similar to a duel between rivals.

♦ **THE BURGTHEATER** The entrance of the main Viennese theater. Besides operatic performances, splendid subscription concertos were held.

♦ **MUZIO CLEMENTI** Great pianist and composer (1752–1832). In 1782, in Vienna, he rivaled Mozart as a piano virtuoso.

♦ **JOHANN ANDREAS STEIN** Piano maker (1728–1792). His instruments were greatly appreciated by Mozart.

♦ **ANTON STADLER** The greatest clarinetist of the eighteenth century (1753–1812). Mozart wrote the *Clarinet Concerto,* K.622, for him.

47

PRAGUE

In Mozart's day, Prague, more than any other city, considered the theater an integral part of life. The artistic activities, especially the musical ones, were based on solid tradition due to the strength of its wind ensemble. Society in Prague was different from that in Vienna, which was so strongly influenced by the court. The modern tastes in Prague explain Mozart's unprecedented success. The opera impresario, Pasquale Bondini, acted as Mozart's client in a more competent and modern way than the Emperor of Austria.

♦ THE VILLA
In the days preceding the performance of *Don Giovanni*, Mozart visited his friends, František Xaver and Josepha Dušek in their country house known as "Villa Bertramka," on the outskirts of Prague.

♦ THE CITY
At the end of the eighteenth century, Prague had a population of nearly 50,000 people. Its cultural life (above all, theatrical and musical) was very animated.

♦ MOZART
The composer is finishing the overture to *Don Giovanni*, which apparently has been written at the last minute and concluded only two days before the opera was to be staged.

♦ **THE THEATER**
The Ständetheater in Prague where *Don Giovanni* was first featured and where *La clemenza di Tito* (*The Clemency of Titus*) was also premiered in 1791. It was built in 1781 according to the wishes of Count Nostiz. In 1984, the movie *Amadeus* was filmed here by Milos Forman.

♦ **JOSEPHA DUŠEK**
Singer (1754–1824). She interpreted the operas of Mozart and Beethoven. It is very likely that Mozart fell in love with her during his stay in Prague.

♦ **FRANTIŠEK DUŠEK**
An excellent harpsichord and piano player, he has left behind a rich symphonic and chamber music collection.

14. MOZART'S LIFE ♦ *On January 8, 1787, Wolfgang and Constanze set off to Prague, where* Figaro *was performed with great success. They then returned to Vienna, where at the end of May, the news of Leopold's death reached them. On October 1, they returned to Prague for the premiere of* Don Giovanni, *which took place on the 29th. In November, they went back to Vienna. On December 27, Theresia, their fourth child was born; she died a few months later. In May, 1788, Don Giovanni was staged in Vienna. Mozart wrote other sublime works, but began to face serious financial difficulties.* ▶

Don Giovanni

In a combination of farce and tragedy never before and never again equaled, Mozart's most celebrated opera recounts the adventures of the noble Spaniard, Don Giovanni, playboy and murderer, symbol of a dissolute and libertine life. Surprised by the Commendant while trying to seduce his daughter, Donna Anna, Giovanni kills him in a duel. He then turns his charms on the noble Donna Elvira and the peasant Zerlina. Everything collapses when Giovanni, at the graveyard where the Commendant is buried, invites his funeral statue to supper. When the marble statue arrives, Giovanni refuses to amend his ruthless ways and is dragged down to Hell.

♦ **The opera history**
Don Giovanni (above, the title page of the first edition of the libretto by Lorenzo da Ponte) was staged for the first time on October 29, 1787, at the Ständetheater in Prague, which had commissioned Mozart to do the opera. Its literary source is the drama *El burlador de Sevilla y el Convivado de piedra* (1630) by the Spaniard Tirso de Molina. The same subject had been reworked by the French writer Molière in 1665, who introduced the role of Don Giovanni's servant. Later, there were many other operatic adaptations. The most striking is *Don Giovanni Tenorio* by Giuseppe Gazzaniga in 1787. After the success in Prague of *The Marriage of Figaro*, *Don Giovanni* marked Mozart's great popularity in the Bohemian capital. The following year, the opera was repeated in Vienna but was not acclaimed in the same triumphant way.

The finale
Don Giovanni has just refused another love offer by Donna Elvira, when he receives the unexpected visit of the Commendant while he is having supper with Leporello.

♦ **Don Giovanni**
Handsome, strong, and valiant, he could be a hero, if only a destructive instinct, which will eventually prove fatal, would not always prevail and ruin him.

♦ **The chorus**
During the finale, a chorus of spirits, singing outside the scene, lists Don Giovanni's faults, sentencing him to eternal damnation. Giovanni, torn but unrepentent, falls into the depths of the earth. Sitting at the table that is still sumptuously set, Leporello, white with fear, is afraid to look at him.

♦ **Under the stage**
The last scene of the opera is perfect for spectacular scenic tricks. Don Giovanni, surrounded by a pit of fire, is swallowed up by the earth and is pulled down a trapdoor, while stagehands use bellows to send up puff clouds of smoke.

♦ **LEPORELLO**
Don Giovanni's servant is a character taken from the world of the *opera buffa*. He nurtures mixed feelings toward his master. He fears his evil nature, but at the same time he admires in him all the qualities that he does not have: vitality, the power to seduce women, and a carefree arrogance.

♦ **DON OTTAVIO**
Donna Anna's betrothed bridegroom, he is a naive, sincere, and faithful man with honest feelings but without his rival's fascination.

♦ **DONNA ELVIRA**
Desperately in love with Don Giovanni, she is constantly rejected and deceived by him but is unable to transform her love into hate.

♦ **THE COMMENDANT**
Donna Anna's old father who represents the moral law that not even Don Giovanni can break.

♦ **MASETTO AND ZERLINA**
A young couple of betrothed peasants. She is malicious and fascinated by the playboy; he is wise, but incapable of freeing his lover from the libertine's clutches.

♦ **THE MUSIC**
Don Giovanni is different from any other work by Mozart. To represent the contrast between traditional characters, such as Leporello and Zerlina (respectively, above and below, in two stage sketches with Don Giovanni), and others outside the common experience (such as the Commendant and Don Giovanni), Mozart resorts to different solutions: those of the *opera buffa*, often charged to the point of losing their spontaneity, and those of the *opera seria*, pushed to the point of creating a type of demonic music. The artist is thus able to illustrate Don Giovanni's vital and destructive force, the psychology of the minor characters, and the supernatural appearance of the Commendant.

♦ **DONNA ANNA**
Seduced by Don Giovanni, she witnesses the libertine killing her father.

♦ **THE STATUE**
A system of pulleys brings the funeral monument of the Commendant to the scene.

FREEMASONRY

The eighteenth century has been called the Age of Reason (or Age of Enlightenment) to emphasize using reason to support the ideals of progress and to learn truth. Although Freemasonry, which originated in London in 1717, adopted a somewhat mystical ritual, it was the first organization that associated freemen under the ideals of progress and moral and spiritual elevation. Artists, men of letters, and political figures became members. Mozart joined the Masons in 1784. Several compositions from his last years contain references to the Masonic principles.

♦ **FREEMASONRY AND REVOLUTION**
Freemasonry, probably dating back to the ancient guild of free master builders from which it had taken its symbols, was feared by governments, which regarded it as the source of a possible subversion of the social order. The activity of its organizations was blocked in those European countries where the Catholic Church was strong, and Masons were excommunicated. They then formed secret local associations called lodges. Mozart joined the Viennese lodge, *Zur Wohltätigkeit* (Beneficence), on December 14, 1784. Above and below, Master Masons' aprons partly embroidered in gold with some Masonic symbols, and the compass that represents God's impartial justice.

♦ **THE COMPASS**
It symbolizes divine justice in the circle that it traces, all the Masonic brothers, and symbolically all mankind.

♦ **THE DISPOSITION**
The layout of the Masonic temple follows very precise rules. On the northern side there are the Apprentices, on the southern side, the superior degrees of the hierarchy, represented by the Fellows and the Masters.

♦ **THE MASTER**
He directs the activity of the lodge and initiates the new brothers. After him, the most important dignitaries are the Wardens, the Orator, the Secretary, and the Treasurer.

♦ **THE INDUCTION**
The novice is appointed Entered Apprentice. He will wear the white apron, the symbol of work.

THE ENVIRONMENT
The lodge is a rectangular room where initiation practices are held. Masons access it through an entrance that is located west of the room, then they proceed east, the brightest point of the room, where the Chair of the Worshipful Master is located.

♦ **MASONIC MUSIC**
Mozart composed several pieces inspired by the ideals of Freemasonry, among them two cantatas in honor of his lodge brothers. One of these was based on a text by Emanuel Schikaneder and the *Mauerische Trauermusik* (Masonic Funeral Music), K.477.

♦ **THE FLOOR**
The checkered floor with its tiles of contrasting colors symbolizes the opposing principles of good and evil that exist in the human soul.

♦ **THE RUG**
It contains all the symbols of Freemasonry, including the square, the trowel, the level, and the plumb line.

15. MOZART'S LIFE ♦ *Between 1788 and 1790 Mozart composed his last three symphonies, his last three string quartets, and his last opera with libretto by da Ponte,* Così fan tutte *(Thus Do All [Women]). Oppressed by debts, he often turned to his Masonic brother, Michael Puchberg, for assistance, and was forced to move into more and more modest houses. The Viennese court seemed to forget him; after the death of Emperor Joseph II, his name was not even considered for the celebrations in honor of the new Emperor Leopold II.* ➢

The Magic Flute

Mozart's last opera is a fantastic fairy tale whose cardinal themes of human fate are symbolized by a story imbued with the values of the Masonic Order. Prince Tamino, fleeing from a serpent, is saved by three women who show him the portrait of Pamina, daughter of the Queen of the Night, imprisoned by Sarastro. With the help of the bird-catcher Papageno and a magic flute, Tamino rushes to save Pamina. When the two arrive in Sarastro's kingdom, they discover that he is not a tyrant, but a wise and enlightened monarch. To be admitted into the new kingdom, they have to pass several difficult tests but, in the end, love rewards them; Tamino can marry Pamina and Papageno finds his Papagena. The evil forces, guided by the Queen of the Night and the evil jailer Monostatos, sink into the depths of the earth. The ideal of brotherhood is revealed—light triumphs over darkness.

♦ **The opera history**
The premiere of *The Magic Flute* took place in the Viennese Theater auf der Wieden on September 30, 1791. The opera, a Singspiel in German, belongs to a genre popular at the time, the so-called *Zauberoper*, in which a "magic" element determines the development of the events. The idea for the opera came to Mozart in March, 1791, from Emanuel Schikaneder (above), his brother in the Viennese Masonic Lodge and director of the Theater auf der Wieden, who also offered his services as a librettist. His main source is the fairy tale, *Lulu, or The Magic Flute* by the German writer Christoph Wieland, composed in 1789. Mozart worked on it uninterruptedly for seven months. The premiere was not well received, but the opera eventually enjoyed lasting and widespread popularity.

The dress rehearsal
Up to the last moment, Mozart, the singers, and the players rehearsed the show with the aid of many helpers.

♦ **A poor theater**
The Theater auf der Wieden, owned by Schikaneder, had neither the fame nor the financial resources of the other large Viennese theaters.

♦ **The scene**
Seated on a throne surrounded by a wide, starry background, the Queen of the Night makes her first appearance by asking Tamino to free her captured daughter.

♦ **The Queen of the Night**
She is a two-faced character. During the first part of the opera, she seems a sympathetic figure, the mother in tears for the loss of her daughter. Later, she reveals her true cruel and vicious nature.

♦ **Mozart**
The composer participated at the rehearsals and personally conducted the first performance.

♦ **Tamino**
The young prince, who wears Japanese costumes, is wise, patient, and strong. Mozart composed some of his most dazzling arias for the prince's tenor voice.

The machines
Schikaneder was a clever impresario. In his theater there were wonderful scenic effects with avant-garde machinery.

♦ **The music**
Even though the music of *The Magic Flute* is sometimes very complex, it is always understandable. It has been said that in *The Magic Flute*, cultured and popular music meet for the last time. Above, the libretto's title page.

♦ **Sarastro**
He is a solemn character, with the deep voice of the bass, considered a sign of wisdom and nobility.

♦ **Pamina**
Pamina, a naïve and sunny girl, dressed very simply. She represents the instinctive tendency toward the good in life, typical of pure creatures.

♦ **Papageno**
He is a docile and not very brave fellow who always carries his bird cage with him.

A PAUPER'S GRAVE

To die alone, without the comfort of deserved recognition, has been the recurrent tragic destiny of many artists. The idea of genius seems to indicate comprehension on the part of the public and great isolation for the artist. In the eighteenth century, musicians were treated as mere craftsmen. Mozart contributed to the dignity of his art, obstinately claiming his own professional and economic independence. He was buried in a pauper's grave, his fate suggesting that the image of the freelance artist had not yet been recognized.

♦ **THE FATAL ILLNESS**
There has been much speculation surrounding the circumstances of Mozart's death. During the nineteenth century, the idea of death by poison had been suggested, and it was suspected that his fierce rival in Vienna, Antonio Salieri (above), was one of the possible perpetrators. Today, this hypothesis has been rejected and almost all the critics believe that Mozart died from natural causes. An American physician (who has also suggested that Mozart suffered from manic-depression), analyzing the history of his illnesses and examining the reports of his last days, has suggested that Mozart died of a streptococcal infection contracted on November 18, 1791, during a meeting of his Masonic lodge. This suggests that it would have been a very sudden illness.

♦ **THE LAST LODGINGS**
The lodgings on the Rauhensteingasse where Mozart died on December 5, 1791.

♦ **THE CEMETERY**
St. Mark's Cemetery, just outside Vienna. The body had been thrown into an unmarked grave. Later efforts to identify the grave were unsuccessful.

♦ A PANORAMIC VIEW OF ST. MARK'S CEMETERY
The Viennese outskirts showing the huge St. Mark's Cemetery where Mozart was buried.

♦ THE CORONATION
On October 9, 1790, Leopold II was crowned Emperor, and the following year, named King of Bohemia. In Prague, Mozart, completely isolated, was not among the composers called to celebrate the event.

♦ JOSEPH II
The Emperor died 22 months before Mozart. During his last years, he was a careless protector, indifferent to Mozart's financial struggles.

16. MOZART'S LIFE ♦ *In March, 1791, Mozart performed in public for the last time. In July, his sixth child, Franz Xaver Wolfgang, was born. Mozart was involved in composing his last operatic masterpieces,* The Clemency of Titus *and* The Magic Flute, *performed on September 6 and 30 in Prague and in Vienna. In October, he was alone in Vienna (his wife was at the spa in Baden). While he was composing the* Requiem, *he suddenly fell ill and was forced into bed on November 20. He died during the night of December 5th and was buried in a common grave in St. Mark's Cemetery.* ♦

The Requiem

At the end of the eighteenth century, a composer could receive commissions to write music from various sources: religious institutions, courts, and theaters, which constantly needed new operas to satisfy the public. The same musicians, through academies and subscription concerts, created social events to sell their own compositions. There were also private clients, generally noble families or rich bourgeois. The case of the *Requiem,* the last of Mozart's masterpieces, is unique in this respect, as the opera was commissioned by a noble landowner who wished to pass it off as his own.

♦ The opera's history

The *Requiem* was commissioned to Mozart in July, 1791, by Johann Sortschan, an agent of Count Franz Walsegg who wanted to pass it off as one of his own works in memory of his late wife. The client was willing to pay in advance and did not set any deadline for the musician. Mozart accepted with apprehension. As Constanze later reported, he felt that he was writing it for his own death, which he thought was imminent. Mozart could not finish the work in time. Fearing that he would lose his fee, Constanze asked her husband's best students to complete the piece and Franz Xaver Süssmayr finished the work. Above, Mozart's monument in Salzburg.

♦ The wife

By selling the *Requiem,* Constanze managed to not lose the income from her husband's last work.

♦ The editor

The *Requiem* was published by Breitkopf & Härtel of Leipzig. Constanze, breaking the agreement with the client, had given the manuscript to the editor.

♦ The student

Süssmayr was very close to Mozart but it is impossible to determine the degree of his personal contribution to Mozart's masterpiece.

♦ **THE MONUMENT**
To honor the memory of his wife, who died in February, 1791, at a young age, Walsegg had commissioned the construction of a monument to her from the renowned Viennese sculptor, Johann Martin Fischer.

♦ **THE MUSIC BUSINESS**
In Mozart's final years, the role of the music publisher became more and more important. Private clients commissioned works from musicians, who later sold them to the publishers to increase their meager incomes. As it was not yet possible to reproduce the actual musical scores, it was necessary to own the scores in order to be able to listen to them. The increase in the number of talented amateurs capable of playing the score of an opera, sonata, or symphony on a piano guaranteed the publisher a satisfactory income. Above, Constanze Mozart, who took charge of her husband's contracts.

♦ **THE CLIENT**
Walsegg was a dilettante violoncellist, with no talent for composing.

THE MYTH

The music, the image, and the name of Mozart have endured for two centuries. His work was a turning point between two eras—the music of a society with its roots in the principles of authority, and the music of our contemporary world. His successors and those who have contributed to making his works known to the world have diligently analyzed his legacy, working from the heritage that he left to future generations. Besides Mozart's contribution to the successive evolution of the history of this art, a myth has grown up around him (in proportions never before and never again to be equaled by another musician) founded on the romantic cult of the genius, a myth that has spread beyond the borders of music to invade distant worlds from rock to films to the world of business.

♦ BEETHOVEN
Ludwig van Beethoven (1770–1827) inherited from Haydn and Mozart the set of rules and codes that exists under the name of *classical style*. The development of this style and the evolution in the Romantic sense are his contribution to the history of music.

♦ HERBERT VON KARAJAN
One of the most distinguished orchestra directors of our time (1908–1989), he was born, as was Mozart, in Salzburg, where he promoted a festival that is today's most prestigious European musical event and where a great deal of space is devoted to works of Mozart.

♦ CHOCOLATE CANDY
In Salzburg, the image of Wolfgang Amadeus Mozart and that of the city itself go together, shown on many commercial products, including a famous brand of chocolate candy.

♦ AMADEUS
This fictional film biography (1984), directed by the American movie director, Milos Forman, starred Tom Hulce as Mozart and was well received.

♦ WEBER
Carl Maria von Weber (1786–1826) is considered the first great German opera composer of the nineteenth century. His masterpieces (especially, *Der Freischütz*) owe a lot to Mozart's teaching on the treatment of the Singspiel.

♦ MENDELSSOHN
Felix Mendelssohn-Bartholdy (1809–1847) is, among all the Romantic composers, the closest one to the ideal of formal equilibrium and natural expressiveness that uses Mozart as his reference point.

♦ MAHLER
Gustav Mahler (1860–1911), orchestra director and composer, is among the most important modern interpreters of Mozart. His lectures on Mozart's works, especially *Don Giovanni,* were exceptional.

♦ STRAVINSKY
Few musicians of the twentieth century have had the creative spontaneity that is attributed to Mozart, but the Russian Igor Stravinsky (1882–1971) can be compared to him for his inventive and compositional dexterity.

♦ BRUNO WALTER
This German orchestra director (1876–1962) was one of the greatest interpreters of Mozart in the twentieth century. His performances of Mozart's operatic and symphonic repertoire remain unforgettable.

♦ ELISABETH SCHWARZKOPF
The German soprano (1915) has interpreted the great feminine roles of the works of Mozart to the highest degree. She has been the Countess in *Le nozze di Figaro*, Donna Elvira in *Don Giovanni*, and Fiordiligi in *Così fan tutte*.

♦ GLENN GOULD
Canadian pianist (1932–1982), who had a large and unconventional repertoire, sometimes gave unusual interpretations of Mozart's sonatas. His opinions on the composer, expressed on television or in magazine articles, are famous.

♦ GLYNDEBOURNE
In Sussex, Great Britain, a festival was created in 1934 dedicated to the music of Amadeus Mozart. It was founded by the orchestra director Fritz Busch (1890–1951), who conducted outstanding performances of the main works of Mozart here.

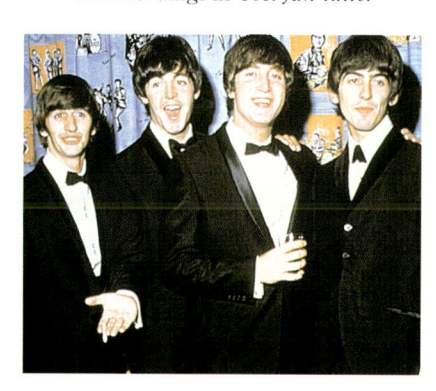

♦ THE BEATLES
It has been said of this British rock band (that so successfully created songs of extraordinary freshness and inventive dexterity) that it occupies in the history of pop music a place similar to that occupied in classical music by Mozart.

INDEX OF MOZART'S WORKS

Mozart was a very prolific composer during his short life. In 1862 the Austrian musicologist Ludwig von Köchel (1800–1877) listed chronologically all of Mozart's works, which came to 626 pieces. He assigned a catalog number preceded by the consonant K, the initial of his last name, to each composition. Later editions of the catalog followed, with changes in some cases in the catalog numbers. The eighth edition is the latest one—1983. Mozart's music, with inevitable variations due to fragments and dubious works, including lost works, amounts to: 18 operas plus stage works, ballets, and incomplete pieces; eight oratorios and cantatas, almost 20 Masses, and 40 sacred pieces, roughly 80 vocal and instrumental compositions; 40 Lieder for song and piano, and 40 canons for voices; more than 50 symphonies (including sketches, dubious, or incomplete works) and almost 30 piano and orchestra concertos; at least seven violin and orchestra concertos, around 20 divertimentos; about ten serenades and three cassations (a composition similar to the serenade and the divertimento); more than 15 church sonatas; 30 trios, quartets, and quintets for strings and piano; around 15 wind compositions; 20 violin and piano sonatas; about 40 sonatas and piano variations; 10 works for four-hand piano and two-piano soli, and various short compositions for instruments.

OPERAS

In the opera genre, Mozart produced many masterpieces, cultivating all the forms of the musical theater that were popular in his time (*opera seria, opera buffa,* and *Singspiel* in German).

His first opera, *Bastien und Bastienne,* **K.50**, composed when he was 12 years old, was inspired by *Le devin du village (The Village Soothsayer),* a story by Jean-Jacques Rousseau. *Mitridate, rè di Ponto (Mithridates, King of Pontus),* **K.87**, after the original text by Racine, composed in 1770 between Bologna and Milan, is a serious opera dating from his first stay in Italy, a work that does not succeed in perfectly blending music and theater. The serious opera *Lucio Silla,* **K.135**, 1772, composed after the success of *Mitridate* for the Milan carnival season of 1772–1773, is a more mature work.

Mozart wrote other splendid operas. *Idomeneo, rè di Creta (Idomeneus, King of Crete),* **K.366**, [see page 28] is a serious opera composed between 1780 and 1781. *Die Entführung aus dem Serail (The Abduction from the Seraglio),* **K.384**, is an *opera buffa* in three acts in German [see page 33], composed between 1781 and 1782. *Le nozze di Figaro (The Marriage of Figaro),* **K.492**, is an *opera buffa* in four acts [see pages 44–45] from 1785–1786, Mozart's first masterpiece in this genre in Italian. *Il Dissoluto punito ossia il Don Giovanni (The Punished Dissolute, or Don Giovanni),* **K.527**, is a drama in two acts [see pages 50–51] from 1787. *Così fan tutte* (literally, *Thus Do All [Women]*), **K.588**, is an *opera buffa* in two acts, commissioned by the Emperor in 1789, and was thought to be inspired by a true story that took place in the Viennese noble ranks. It had been ignored during the entire nineteenth century. Its libretto was called a banal inheritance of the *commedia dell'arte* and its music appeared to be a pale remake of *The Marriage of Figaro.* Our century has reevaluated it as an enchanting blend of poetry and music. *Die Zauberflöte (The Magic Flute),* **K.620**, is a Singspiel in two acts of 1791 [see pages 54–55]. *La clemenza di Tito (The Clemency of Titus),* **K. 621**, is a serious opera in two acts, again from 1791, with a libretto by Caterino Mazzola and inspired by an old text by Metastasio. It was composed for the coronation of Leopold II as King of Bohemia. His contemporaries found the transposition in music too cold from a text that was so inventive and full of humanitarian values.

SACRED MUSIC

In the genre of sacred or religious music, the following works are listed in chronological order: The *Missa solemnis* in C minor, **K.139**, was composed by the 12-year-old Mozart for the dedication of a church and directed by him in Vienna in front of the Viennese court. The motet, *Exsultate, jubilate* in F major, **K.165**, was composed at 17 in Milan during his free time between the rehearsals of the opera *Lucio Silla.* The *Krönungsmesse (Missa* in C major, "Coronation"), **K.317**, was written at 23 on his trip from Paris to Salzburg, again in the service of the Archbishop Colloredo.

The church sonatas, like the **K.336** in C major, were short compositions designed to be performed during the mass between the Gloria and Credo, following the Italian custom of enriching the liturgy with instrumental inserts. The *Missa* in C major, **K.337**, was composed at 24 during a period of psychological problems. *The Vesperae solemnes de confessore* in C major, **K.339**, were conceived in 1780. They are five psalms that end the production of the sacred works of the Salzburg years and, because of the presence of composed elements, constitute one of his most remarkable sacred works. The exquisite *Missa* in C minor, **K.427**, dates back to his last trip to Salzburg (1783). The motet, *Ave verum corpus* in D major, **K.618**, of June 18, 1791, was intended for the celebration of the Feast of Corpus Christi, suppressed by Joseph II and reintroduced by his successor Leopold II. Finally, the *Requiem* in D minor, **K.626**, his last work, was written at the end of his life [see pages 58–59].

VOCAL MUSIC

Many of Mozart's glorious works belong to the vocal repertoire. The French arietta *Oiseaux, si tous les ans (Birds, if every year)* in C major, **K.307**, was composed by Mozart for the young singer Augusta, daughter of the flutist Johann Baptist Wendling, a musician in the Mannheim orchestra. The aria for soprano *Io non chiedo eterni dei* in C major, **K.316**, listed in the later editions of the catalog in the Parisian period of 1778, was an homage to the voice of the singer Aloysia Weber. The cantata *Die Maurerfreude (The Mason's Joy),* **K.471**, in E-flat major was intended to celebrate the title of "Knight of the Realm" of the Mason Ignaz von Born for his scientific discoveries. The aria for voices *Non temer, amato bene* in B-flat major, **K.490**, was composed on March 10, 1789, together with the duet for voices *Spiegarti non poss'io* in A major, **K.489**, for the private performance of *Idomeneo* in the palace of Prince Johann Adam Auersperg. The Lied *Abendempfindung* in F major, **K.523**, was composed by Mozart in June 1787, a few weeks after his father's death. It is, therefore, pervaded by a strong feeling of melancholy and sorrow with themes that are more romantic than classic. Its inseparable twin is *An Chloe* in E-flat major, **K.524**, certainly lighter in theme (a promise of love and faithfulness) and in musical writing. The Canon for voices, *Ave Maria* in F major, **K.554**, of September 1788, is part of a group of multi-voice "exercises" that Mozart composed during his free time for no particular occasion or performance. Two canons belong to this group: *Difficile lectu, mihi Mars* in F major, **K.559**, a spirited, jolly, and licentious composition played behind the back of the Viennese tenor Johann Nepomuk Peyerl, famous for a speech defect, and *Bona nox, bist a rechta Ox* in A major, **K.561**, a strange text that refers to the familiar habit in Mozart's house of saying good night ("bona nox"). The bizarre quartet for voices *Caro mio Druck und Schluck* in E-flat major, **K.571a**, is a Viennese piece from the beginning of 1789. Only a fragment of about 50 measures has survived, crammed with word jokes and Italian and Viennese dialect nonsense, perhaps meant to amuse a friendly gathering at the von Joacquin household. The aria for soprano *"Vado, ma dove?"* in E-flat major, **K.583**, was composed in October, 1789, together with the aria *Chi sà, chi sà, qual sia,* in C major, **K.582**, for the soprano Louise Villeneuve. The Lied *Sehnsucht nach dem Frühlinge* in F major, **K.596**, was composed in January 1791, with two other Lieder, for the ballroom music of the Vienna carnival season.

As for the vocal compositions with a Masonic influence, the *Eine kleine Freimaurerkantate (A Little Masonic Cantata)* in C major, **K.623**, is Mozart's last evidence of his Masonic faith. It is a hymn to hope, brotherly love, and solidarity.

SYMPHONIES

Among others, the following symphonies are part of Mozart's symphonic repertoire: the Symphony in A major, **K.201**, from April 6, 1774, generally considered by critics as a transitional composition between the Haydnian and the "gallant" styles that would characterize Mozart until his departure for Paris. The Symphony in D major, "Paris," **No. 31, K.297**, was composed between May and June, 1778, for the Parisian audiences whose competence was, in Mozart's opinion, not too striking, to say the least. The Symphony Concertante in E-flat major, **K.297b**, is dated April, 1778 (the authenticity of the score has been questioned because the manuscript is missing). The Symphony in B-flat major, **No. 33, K.319**, was composed in July, 1779, on his way home after the experience in Paris. The Symphony in C major, **No. 34, K.338**, from almost the same period as the **K.319**, is a gay and ebullient piece. The Symphony Concertante in E-flat major, **K.364**, for violin and viola, was composed between August and September, 1779. The Symphony in D major, "Haffner," **No. 35, K.385**, from summer, 1782, composed to celebrate an important event in the life of the Haffner family, opens the series of the last Viennese symphonies. The Symphony in C major, "Linz," **No. 36, K.425**, composed in only four days between the end of October and the beginning of November 1783, is one of his most famous symphonies, inspired by J. Haydn's works, but with original accents. The Symphony in D major, "Prague," **No. 38, K.504**, dedicated in December, 1786, to the town where *The Marriage of Figaro* had triumphed, is an example of a Viennese symphony with an Italian opera origin. His last great symphonies were composed during the summer of 1788, after the modest success of *Don Giovanni* in Vienna. They are: the Symphony in E-flat major, **No. 39, K.543**, half-way between the effervescence of *Don Giovanni* and the bewitchment of *The Marriage of Figaro;* the Symphony in G minor, **No. 40, K.550**, absolutely one of his most exquisite creations; and, finally, the Symphony in C major, "Jupiter," **No. 41, K.551**, was named by an unknown editor for its exquisite perfection and sophisticated blending of different languages.

ORCHESTRAL MUSIC

The Serenade in D major, "Haffner," **No. 7, K.250**, dates from the Salzburg years, between March, 1775, and September, 1777, and was intended for the wedding of a lady of the local aristocracy. The Serenade in D major, "Posthorn," **No. 9, K.320**, from August, 1779, is a work of minor ambition composed after the long trip to Mannheim and Paris. The *Maurerische Trauermusik (Masonic Funeral Music)* in C minor, **K.477**, from 1785 in commemoration of two Masons who had died, is influenced by the Masons' values. The divertimento, *Ein musikalischer Spass (A Musical Joke)* in F major, **K.522**, composed during a break from writing *Don Giovanni,* can be considered a parody of the musical compositions of minor musicians with astounding errors and daring matching tonalities. The serenade *Eine kleine Nachtmusik (A Little Night Music)* in G major, **No. 13, K.525**, was also composed during the summer of 1787 and is one of the most often performed pieces in all of Mozart's repertoire.

CONCERTOS AND PIANO MUSIC

Mozart wrote many instrumental concertos. Three notable violin concertos are the Violin Concerto in G major, **No. 3, K.216**; the Violin Concerto in D major, **No. 4, K.218**; and the Violin Concerto in A major, "Turkish," **No. 5, K.219**, all composed between September and December, 1775, and considered unsurpassed examples of that "gallant music" of which serenades and divertimentos had been the messengers. The Flute and Harp Concerto in C major, **K.299**, is among Mozart's earliest Parisian works. His greatest concerto for two pianos soli is considered the Double Piano Concerto in E-flat major, **No. 10, K.365**, from the beginning of 1779, conceived probably for himself and for his sister Nannerl as a souvenir of their tours around the world as young artists. The Piano Concerto in E-flat major, "Jeunehomme," **No. 9, K.271**, from January, 1777, owes its name to a French keyboard player passing through Salzburg who had made a strong impression on the composer. Mozart's great genius shines in a series of piano sonatas composed in Paris in the summer of 1778. The **K.331**, with the famed "Turkish" finale, is one of them. At the top of his piano production are 14 concertos composed between 1782 and 1786. The Piano Concerto in F major **No. 11, K.413**, was composed during the winter of 1782 for the Viennese audience, together with the Piano Concerto in A major **No. 12, K.414**, and the Piano Concerto in C major **No. 13, K.415**. These three concertos are close to the musical *esprit* of Johann Christian Bach. In 1784 alone, Mozart wrote six concertos: the Piano Concerto in E-flat major **No. 14, K.449**; the **No. 15, K.450**, in B-flat major; the **No. 16, K.451**, in D major; the **No. 17, K.453**, in G major; the **No. 18, K.456**, in B-flat major; and the **No. 19, K.459**, in F major. The capability of musical development of the solo instrument in its always balanced relationship with the orchestra is simple and impressive. From 1785 are the very famous **No. 20, K.466**, in D minor, peculiar for the dark first and last movements; the **No. 21, K.467**, in C major; and the **No. 22, K.482**, in E-flat major. The **No. 23, K.488**, in A major, one of his most illustrious and labored works, was composed in the spring of 1786 at the same time as the last pages of *The Marriage of Figaro*. The **No. 24, K.491**, in C minor and the **No. 25, K.503**, in C major, from March and December 1786, end the cycle of the 12 concertos from the period 1784–1786. The *Kronüngskonzert (Coronation Concerto)* **No. 26, K.537**, in D major from 1788—the title comes from a later performance for the coronation of the Emperor Leopold II of Habsburg—and the **No. 27, K.595**, in B-flat major, from 1791, are his last two piano concertos.

CHAMBER MUSIC

The Quintet for Piano and Winds in E-flat major, **K.452**, from the end of March, 1784, is considered his most exquisite example of chamber music for wind instruments. The String Quintet in C major, **K.515**, and the String Quintet in G minor, **K.516**, are glorious. They are masterpieces of chamber music for all times composed by Mozart in the spring of 1787. A piece of miraculous formal equilibrium is the *"Stadler Quintett"* in A major, **K.581**, for clarinet and strings, composed in September, 1789, during a time of human and artistic solitude. The String Quintet in D major, **K.593**, opens the way to the masterpieces of Mozart's last years. The String Quintet in E-flat major, **K.614**, contemporary to the first part of *The Magic Flute,* can be associated with it. The six string quartets written between the end of 1782 and the beginning of 1785, dedicated to Joseph Haydn, are brilliant. They are the String Quartet in G major, **K.387**; the **K.421**, in D minor; the **K.428**, in E-flat major called *Jagd* (Hunting); the **K.458**, in B-flat major; the **K.464**, in A major; and the **K.465**, known as "the Dissonance," in C major. The String Quartet in D major, **K.499**, is the only one that does not belong to a cycle. Three quartets, the **K.575**, in D major, the **K.589**, and the **K.590**, were commissioned by King Frederick William II of Prussia during Mozart's journey to the north of Germany between April and June, 1789. The Trio **K.542**, in E major and the **K.564**, in G major, both for piano and strings, composed in the summer of 1788, belong to a group of lesser-known works that were written for family gatherings.

MUSIC FOR WOODWINDS

The first wind solo concerto is the Bassoon Concerto in B-flat major, **K.191**, from June, 1774, when the composer was back in Salzburg after his trips to Italy. The two Flute Concertos **K.313** and **K.314**, respectively in G major and in D major, were composed between January and February, 1778, for an occasional client. The serenade for 13 instruments, "Gran Partita," **K.361**, from February–April, 1778, is regarded as one of the greatest pieces for soli flutes in the entire history of music. With the clarinet concerto in A major, **K.622**, from October, 1791, back from Prague where he had gone for the performance of *The Clemency of Titus,* Mozart created his last work for a solo instrument, the clarinet and orchestra.

General Index

A
Aachen 8
Alembert, Jean-Baptiste Le Rond 35
Amati, Andrea 37
Anfossi, Pasquale 21
Arco, Karl 5
Artaria, Carlo 16
Artaria & Co. 16, 30
Attwood, Thomas 39
Augsburg 8
Austria 4, 10

B
Baden 57
Bach, Johann Christian 5, 8, 12, 22
Bach, Johann Sebastian 5
Beatles 61
Beaumarchais, Pierre-Augustin Caron de 43, 44
Beethoven, Ludwig van 9, 24, 40, 49, 60
Berchtold zu Sonnenburg, Baron 6
Bohemia 57
Bologna 13
   Accademia Filarmonica 12, 13
Bondini, Pasquale 48
Bonn 8
Breitkopf & Härtel 58
Bretzner, Friedrich 33
Brünn 11
Brussels 8
Busch, Fritz 61

C
Caldara, Antonio 12
Catherine II of Russia 8
Ceneda 42
Charles V of Lorraine 32
Cimarosa, Domenico 12, 20
Clement XIV, Pope 13
Clementi, Muzio 12, 47
Colloredo, Hieronymus von 4, 10, 11, 16, 35
Cologne 8, 19
Corelli, Arcangelo 13
Cristofori, Bartolomeo 14, 15

D
da Ponte, Lorenzo 5, 42, 43, 44, 50, 53
Diderot, Denis 35
Dittersdorf, Karl Ditters von 36
Dušek, Fratišek Xaver 48, 49
Dušek, Josepha 4, 48, 49

E
Eisenstadt 25
Esterház 24, 25
Esterházy, family of 24
Esterházy, Paul Anton 24
Esterházy, Nicolaus 24, 25

F
Farinelli, Carlo 13
Feo, Francesco 21
Florence 9, 13, 14
Fisher, Johann Martin 59
Forman, Milos 49, 60
France 9, 11, 41
Frederick II of Prussia 8

G
Galuppi, Balsassarre 20
Gazzaniga, Giuseppe 50
Gefels, Franz 32
Glyndebourne 61
Gluck, Christoph Willibald von 5, 22, 23
Goethe, Wolfgang Johann 8
Gould, Glenn 61
Great Britain 61
Grimm, Friedrich Melchior 22, 23
Guarneri, Giuseppe 37

H
Händel, Georg Friedrich 12
Hapsburg 8
Haydn, Franz Joseph 5, 16, 24, 25, 26, 27, 30, 34, 36, 40, 60
Haydn, Johann Michael 5
Heidelberg 8
Holland 8, 11
Huberty 16
Hulce, Tom 60
Hungary 24

I
Isabel of Parma 9, 42
Italy 12, 13, 16, 37

J
Jommelli, Niccolò 21
Joseph II of Austria 4, 8, 9, 30, 31, 32, 42, 44, 48, 53, 57

K
Kahlenberg 32
Karajan, Herbert von 60

L
Lange, Joseph 28
Leipzig 58
Leopold II of Austria 53, 57
Linley, Thomas 9
Linz 35, 39
Lisbon 12
London 6, 8, 12, 22, 24, 52
Lotter, Johann Jakob 16
Louis XVI, King of France 43

M
Mahler, Gustav 61
Mainz 8
Mannheim 8, 22, 23, 25, 39
Mantua 13
Maria Theresa of Austria, Empress 4, 8, 9, 28
Marie Antoinette, Queen of France 9
Martini, Giambattista 5, 12, 42
Maximilian, Prince Elector 6
Mendelssohn-Bartholdy, Felix 61
Metastasio, Pietro 42
Milan 12, 13, 16
Mödlhammer, Johannes Ferdinand 25
Molière, Jean-Baptiste 50
Munich 6, 8, 25, 28, 29, 31
   Court Theater 28
   National Theater 29
Mozart, Carl Thomas 39
Mozart, Franz Alois 16, 17
Mozart, Franz Xaver 57
Mozart, Johann Thomas Leopold 42
Mozart, Leopold 4, 6, 7, 8, 10, 16, 23, 39, 49
Mozart, Maria Anna (Nannerl) 4, 6
Mozart, Raimund Leopold 35
Mozart, Thekla Maria Anna 4, 16, 17
Mozart, Theresia 49
Mozart, Weber Constanze 4, 31, 32, 35, 38, 49, 58, 59

N
Nancy 25
Naples 12, 31
Nostiz, Count 49

O
Olmütz 11
opera buffa 23, 42, 45, 51, 52
opera comica 12, 20, 23, 28, 33, 44
opera seria 12, 20, 21, 22, 28, 52
Orsini-Rosenberg, Count 30, 31

P
Paisiello, Giovanni 12, 20
Paris 7, 8, 11, 16, 18, 22, 23, 25, 31, 44
Paris Opéra 23
Pergolesi, Giovan Battista 20, 23
Pertl, Anna Maria 4, 6, 7, 22
Piccinni, Niccolò 20, 22
Ployer, Barbara 38
Prague 4, 44, 48, 49, 50, 57
   Ständetheater 49, 50
   Villa Bertramka 48
Puchberg, Michael 5, 53

R
Rohrau 24
Rome 13
Rousseau, Jean-Jacques 42
Ruckers, Hans 14

S
Salieri, Antonio 5, 12, 30, 31, 39, 42, 56
Salzburg 4, 6, 7, 10, 11, 13, 16, 18, 25, 31, 35, 58, 60
   Cathedral 11
Sammartini, Giuseppe 12
St. Petersburg 12
Scarlatti, Alessandro 12
Schachtner, Johann Andreas 7
Schantz, Johann 30
Schantz, Wenzel 30
Schikaneder, Emanuel 5, 53, 54, 55
Schrattenbach, Sigismud von 13
Schwarzkopf, Elisabeth 61
Schwetzingen 8
Sienese, (known as) Giusto Ferdinando Tenducci 22
Soler, Antonio 42
Sortschan, Johann 58
Stadler, Anton 47
Stein, Johann Andreas 47
Stephanie, Gottlieb 30, 31, 33
Stradivari, Antonio 37
Strasbourg 25
Stravinsky, Igor 61
Sussex 61
Süssmayr, Franz Xaver 5, 39, 58
Switzerland 11

T
Tasso, Torquato 21
Teatro Regio 21
Thurn und Taxis, Count 6
Tirso de Molina, (known as) Gabriel Téllez 50
Tonkünstler-Societät 30
Torricella, family of 16, 30
Traetta, Tommaso 12, 21
Turin 21

U
United States 42

V
Van Swieten, Gottfried 5
Vanhal, Johann Baptist 36
Varesco, abbé 28
Venice 12
Verona 13
Vienna 4, 5, 8, 10, 11, 12, 16, 22, 24, 30, 31, 32, 34, 35, 38, 39, 42, 43, 44, 47, 49, 50, 56, 57
   Belvedere 35
   Burgtheater 30, 31, 32, 42, 44, 47
   St. Stephen's Cathedral 24
   Freyung 32
   German National Theater (see Burgtheater)
   Historisches Museum der Stadt 32
   Hofburg 31
   Höhe Brücke 38
   Kärntnerthor 30
   Michaelerplatz 30
   Prater 34
   Rauhensteingasse 56
   Riding School 31
   Saint Peter's Church 35
   Schönbrunn 8, 9, 42
   Schottenkirche 33
   St. Mark's Cemetery 56, 57
   St. Michael's Church 30
   Theater auf der Wieden 5, 54
Vittorio Veneto (see Ceneda)
Vivaldi, Antonio 12
Von Kahlenberg, Count 32

W
Wladstätten, Maria Elizabeth 38
Walsegg, Franz von 58, 59
Walter, Anton 30
Walter, Bruno 61
Weber, Aloysia 4, 23, 25, 28, 31, 39
Weber, Cäcilia 31
Weber, Carl Maria von 61
Weber, Family 25
Wieland, Christoph Martin 43, 54

Z
Zanotti, Camillo 12
Zeno, Apostolo 21
Zur Wohltätigkeit (Masonic Lodge) 52